Relentless Pursuit

The Ultimate Guide to Managing Distressed Hotel & Resort Assets

Stephen Nalley DBA, CHA

Dedication

To my ESJ Towers Team in Puerto Rico lead by Maritza Vicente, Huascar A. Polanco, Dania Cruz, David Garcia, Edgardo Cabrera, Jaime Vazquez, Jose Nieves, Leslie Montes, Melvin Ramos, Nancy Velez, Wing Fung, Alba Agosto, Jeremy Diaz and Carolina Pizarro. Your tireless dedication to the foundations and principles in this body of work demonstrates that not only can distressed assets be revived, but more importantly that there is no substitution for teamwork and passion.

Acknowledgment

I would like to express my sincere gratitude to Marcia Brinton, a truly remarkable and invaluable executive who has been by my side throughout my entire career in managing distressed hotel assets.

From the very beginning, Marcia has provided me with unwavering support and guidance, always believing in my abilities and pushing me to achieve my full potential. Her vast knowledge and organizational skills have been instrumental in assisting me in building the Inner Circle and Black Briar Companies. I am forever grateful for her mentorship and leadership.

Through the many challenges and triumphs, we have faced together, Marcia has been a constant source of inspiration and motivation, never hesitating to lend a helping hand or offer words of encouragement when I needed them most. Her unwavering dedication and commitment to excellence have been an inspiration to me, and I am honored to have had the opportunity to work alongside such an exceptional professional and leader.

I am deeply grateful for Marcia's tireless efforts and steadfast support, which have been instrumental in my professional growth and success. Her vision, passion, and unwavering commitment to excellence have been invaluable to the success that our organization has achieved, and I am truly fortunate to have had the privilege of working with her.

Thank you, Marcia, for your support, guidance, and friendship over the years. Your contributions have been immeasurable, and I am grateful for all that you have done for me and out organization. I will always remember and cherish our time together, and I wish you all the best in your future endeavors.

CONTENTS

Chapter 1:   Financial Analysis

Chapter 2:   Turnaround Plan

Chapter 3:   Market Analysis

Chapter 4:   Target Market

Chapter 5:   Renovations

Chapter 6:   Training

Chapter 7:   Amenities & Services

Chapter 8:   Marketing Efforts

Chapter 9:   Online Reputation

Chapter 10:   Local Businesses

Chapter 11:   Packages & Promotions

Chapter 12:   Loyalty Programs

Chapter 13:   Cost Reductions

Chapter 14:   Operational Efficiency

About the Author

Stephen Nalley is an Entrepreneur, Veteran, Author, Mentor and Founder of the Black Briar Hotel Group and Black Briar Advisors. Black Briar is a uniquely positioned full service real estate investment company that specializes in the acquisition, repositioning, renovating and asset management of distressed hotel & resort assets. Black Briar and its Managing Principles have significant transactional experience and are experts in all phases of the real estate life cycle. This includes deal structuring, contract negotiation, due diligence, underwriting, raising and closing on debt/equity capital structures, asset management, renovations and property management. Black Briar and its principals have owned and asset managed over $2B in real estate assets, which includes over 100 hotel & resort assets.

Prior to Founding Black Briar, Mr. Nalley was the Chief Operating Officer and Chairman of the Executive Committee for Ocean Waters. Ocean Waters was a multifaceted real estate investment company, which consisted of over 129 separate entities, 79 real estate assets, 45 operating hotels, and various office, retail, and residential components. Mr. Nalley was responsible for the day-to-day leadership and general management of the company. Mr. Nalley assisted Ocean Waters and its Principals in creating over $1 Billion in value by acquiring nonperforming Hotel & Resort assets and leading them to profitability.

Prior to his civilian career, Stephen Nalley served in the United States Army as a light infantry squad leader and Commando with the 10th Mountain Division's Special Troops Battalion. Mr. Nalley was honorably discharged and is a disabled service-connected veteran.

Stephen Nalley received a Bachelor of Science Degree in Healthcare Administration from the University of

North Florida, and earned his MBA and DBA from the University of Atlanta and a Law Degree from Washington University School of Law.

Stephen is also a Certified Hotel Administrator through the American Hotel & Lodging Association.

Page Blank Intentionally

Preface

The hospitality industry has always been a challenging and dynamic field, with constant fluctuations in demand, supply, and consumer behavior. Despite the ups and downs, hotels have been an essential part of the global economy, providing jobs, generating revenue, and promoting tourism. However, the COVID-19 pandemic has tested the resilience of the hotel industry like never before. The sudden and severe impact of the pandemic on travel and tourism has resulted in widespread distress and financial hardship for hotel owners and operators.

In such times, managing distressed hotel assets has become a critical skill for hospitality professionals. This book is a comprehensive guide for those who are responsible for managing and turning around financially distressed hotels. It is aimed at owners, operators, asset managers, investors, lenders, and other stakeholders who seek to understand the complexities of hotel distress, and the strategies and tools to overcome it.

The book covers a wide range of topics, from understanding the root causes of hotel distress to devising a recovery plan, and executing it effectively. It provides practical insights into the key challenges of hotel distress, such as cash flow management, debt restructuring, labor costs, and brand value. The book also discusses various legal and regulatory aspects of hotel distress, such as bankruptcy, foreclosure, receivership, and insolvency.

The author of this book brings a wealth of experience and expertise in the hospitality industry, having worked with distressed hotels in various parts of the world. He shares his insights and best practices in managing distressed hotel assets, drawing on real-life case studies and examples. He also provides a range of tools and templates that can be used to analyze, evaluate, and manage distressed hotels effectively.

Managing distressed hotel assets is not just about financial engineering or cost-cutting. It requires a holistic approach that takes into account the needs and expectations of various stakeholders, such as employees, customers, suppliers, and local communities. This book provides a framework for such an approach, emphasizing the importance of communication, collaboration, and creativity in dealing with hotel distress.

We hope that this book will be a valuable resource for anyone involved in managing distressed hotel assets, and that it will contribute to the recovery and growth of the hospitality industry in the post-pandemic world.

Chapter 1

Conduct a Thorough Analysis of the Property's Financials

The first step in turning around a distressed hotel is to conduct a comprehensive analysis of the property's financials. This includes a review of the income statement, balance sheet, and cash flow statement. By analyzing the financial data, the owner can identify the areas of the property that are performing well and those that are not. This information can be used to develop a strategy for turning the hotel around.

Example: The Hyatt Regency Atlanta suffered from low occupancy rates and declining revenues. The owner conducted a thorough analysis of the property's financials and identified several areas that were causing the problems, such as poor customer service and outdated amenities. The owner developed a strategy to address these issues and was able to increase occupancy rates and revenues.

A comprehensive analysis of a hotel's financial statements is a critical task for owners, investors, and managers to understand the financial health of the business. Financial statements, including the balance sheet, income statement, and cash flow statement, provide valuable insights into the hotel's financial position, performance, and cash flows. Analyzing these statements can help identify areas of concern and reasons for financial instability, which can guide decision-making and strategy development. In this chapter, we will discuss how to conduct a comprehensive analysis of a hotel's financial statements and use the data to find areas of concern and reasons for financial instability.

Step 1: Collect Financial Statements

The first step in analyzing a hotel's financial statements is to collect them. The three primary financial statements are the balance sheet, income statement, and cash flow statement. The balance sheet shows the hotel's assets, liabilities, and equity at a specific point in time. The income statement shows the hotel's revenues, expenses, and net income over a period, typically a year. The cash flow statement shows the hotel's cash inflows and outflows over a period.

To obtain these statements, one can contact the hotel's accounting department or retrieve them from the hotel's website, if available. It is essential to collect financial statements for at least three years to have a better understanding of the hotel's financial history and performance trends.

Step 2: Analyze the Balance Sheet

The balance sheet provides a snapshot of the hotel's financial position at a specific point in time. It includes the hotel's assets, liabilities, and equity. Analyzing the balance sheet can help identify areas of concern and reasons for financial instability. The following are some key ratios that can be calculated from the balance sheet:

a) Current Ratio: The current ratio is calculated by dividing current assets by current liabilities. It indicates the hotel's ability to pay its short-term obligations. A current ratio of 1 or higher is considered good.

b) Debt-to-Equity Ratio: The debt-to-equity ratio is calculated by dividing total liabilities by shareholder's equity. It indicates the amount of debt financing relative to equity financing. A higher debt-to-equity ratio indicates a higher risk of financial instability.

c) Working Capital: Working capital is calculated by subtracting current liabilities from current assets. It indicates the hotel's ability to meet its short-term obligations. Positive working capital is a good sign.

d) Fixed Asset Turnover Ratio: The fixed asset turnover ratio is calculated by dividing revenue by fixed assets. It indicates how efficiently the hotel is using its fixed assets to generate revenue.

Step 3: Analyze the Income Statement

The income statement provides information on the hotel's revenues, expenses, and net income over a period. Analyzing the income statement can help identify areas of concern and reasons for financial instability. The following are some key ratios that can be calculated from the income statement:

a) Gross Profit Margin: The gross profit margin is calculated by dividing gross profit by revenue. It indicates the percentage of revenue that is left after deducting the cost of goods sold.

b) Net Profit Margin: The net profit margin is calculated by dividing net income by revenue. It indicates the percentage of revenue that is left after deducting all expenses, including taxes and interest.

c) Operating Expense Ratio: The operating expense ratio is calculated by dividing operating expenses by revenue. It indicates the percentage of revenue that is spent on operating expenses.

d) Return on Assets: The return on assets is calculated by dividing net income by total assets. It indicates how efficiently the hotel is using its assets to generate profits.

Step 4: Analyze the Cash Flow Statement

The cash flow statement provides information on the hotel's cash inflows and outflows over a period. Analyzing the cash flow statement can help identify areas of concern and reasons for financial instability. The following are some key ratios that can be calculated from the cash flow statement:

a) Cash Flow from Operations Ratio: The cash

flow from operations ratio is calculated by dividing cash flow from operations by revenue. It indicates how much cash is generated from the hotel's operations relative to its revenue.

b) Cash Flow Coverage Ratio: The cash flow coverage ratio is calculated by dividing cash flow from operations by total debt. It indicates the hotel's ability to generate cash from its operations to cover its debt obligations.

c) Free Cash Flow: Free cash flow is calculated by subtracting capital expenditures from cash flow from operations. It indicates how much cash is left after deducting capital expenditures to reinvest in the business or pay dividends.

Step 5: Identify Areas of Concern

After analyzing the financial statements and calculating key ratios, the next step is to identify areas of concern. Areas of concern could include declining revenue or profitability, increasing debt levels, low liquidity, and inefficient use of assets. For example, a declining gross profit margin may indicate that the hotel's cost of goods sold is increasing, or its pricing strategy is not effective. An increasing debt-to-equity ratio may indicate that the hotel is relying too much on debt financing, which could lead to financial instability if interest rates rise.

Step 6: Determine Reasons for Financial Instability

Once areas of concern have been identified, the next step is to determine the reasons for financial instability. The reasons for financial instability could be internal or external. Internal reasons could include poor management, inefficient operations, high overhead costs, or ineffective marketing strategies. External reasons could include changes in the economy, increased competition, or changes in consumer preferences.

For example, if the hotel's revenue is declining, the reasons could be due to changes in the local market, a decrease in tourism, or ineffective marketing strategies. If the hotel has high overhead costs, the reasons could be due to inefficient operations, poor management, or outdated technology.

Step 7: Develop a Strategy

After identifying areas of concern and reasons for financial instability, the final step is to develop a strategy to address them. The strategy could include cost-cutting measures, marketing initiatives, improving operations, or developing new revenue streams. It is essential to prioritize the strategies based on their potential impact on the hotel's financial stability and their feasibility.

For example, if the hotel's revenue is declining due to changes in the local market, the strategy could be to diversify its customer base by targeting new markets or developing new products or services that appeal to a broader audience. If the hotel has high overhead costs due to inefficient operations, the strategy could be to streamline operations, reduce waste, or implement new technology to improve efficiency.

In conclusion, conducting a comprehensive analysis of a hotel's financial statements is essential to understand its financial health and identify areas of concern and reasons for financial instability. The analysis should include the balance sheet, income statement, and cash flow statement, and key ratios should be calculated to assess the hotel's liquidity, profitability, and efficiency. Identifying areas of concern and reasons for financial instability is crucial to develop a strategy to address them, which could include cost-cutting measures, marketing initiatives, improving operations, or developing new revenue streams. By conducting a thorough analysis and developing a sound strategy, hotels can improve their financial stability and position themselves for long-term success.

Chapter 2

Develop a Comprehensive Turnaround Plan

Once the analysis of the property's financials is complete, the owner should develop a comprehensive turnaround plan that addresses the issues identified during the analysis. The plan should include specific actions that will be taken to improve the property's financial performance.

Example: The Ritz Carlton in St. Louis developed a comprehensive turnaround plan that included renovating the property's guest rooms, upgrading the restaurant and bar, and increasing the hotel's marketing efforts. As a result, the hotel was able to increase its occupancy rates and revenues.

A turnaround plan is a comprehensive and strategic approach to reviving a struggling business. It involves identifying the root causes of the problem and developing solutions to address them. Turnaround plans are critical for businesses that are facing financial distress, operational inefficiencies, or declining market share. In this chapter, we will discuss how to develop and implement a comprehensive turnaround plan. We will begin by discussing the key elements of a successful turnaround plan and then move on to the steps involved in its development and implementation.

Key Elements of a Successful Turnaround Plan

A successful turnaround plan should address the root causes of the problem and be tailored to the specific needs of the business. There are several key elements that should be included in any comprehensive turnaround plan:

1. A clear diagnosis of the problem: This involves identifying the root causes of the problem, such as financial mismanagement, operational inefficiencies, or declining market share. A clear diagnosis of the problem is essential for developing effective solutions.
2. A realistic assessment of the business's current state: This involves assessing the current financial, operational, and market performance of the business. A realistic assessment is critical

for developing realistic solutions that address the underlying issues.

3. A clear and measurable goal: This involves setting a clear and measurable goal for the business, such as achieving profitability, increasing market share, or improving operational efficiency. The goal should be specific, achievable, and aligned with the overall business strategy.

4. A well-defined strategy: This involves developing a well-defined strategy for achieving the goal. The strategy should be based on the strengths and weaknesses of the business and should be aligned with the overall business strategy.

5. A detailed action plan: This involves developing a detailed action plan for implementing the strategy. The action plan should include specific steps, timelines, and responsibilities.

6. A monitoring and evaluation framework: This involves developing a monitoring and evaluation framework to track progress and make necessary adjustments. The framework should include key performance indicators (KPIs) and regular progress reports.

Development of a Comprehensive Turnaround Plan

The development of a comprehensive turnaround plan involves several steps, including:

Step 1: Conduct a thorough analysis of the business

The first step in developing a comprehensive turnaround plan is to conduct a thorough analysis of the business. This involves gathering and analyzing data on the business's financial performance, operational efficiency, and market position. The analysis should identify the root causes of the problem and highlight areas that require improvement.

For example, if the business is experiencing financial distress, the analysis should identify the sources of the problem, such as high debt levels, low profitability, or poor cash flow management. If the business is experiencing operational inefficiencies, the analysis should identify areas of waste, bottlenecks, or inefficiencies in processes.

Step 2: Set a clear and measurable goal

The next step is to set a clear and measurable goal for the business. The goal should be aligned with the overall business strategy and should be specific, achievable, and time-bound. For example, if the business is experiencing financial distress, the goal may be to achieve profitability within the next 12 months. If the business is experiencing operational inefficiencies, the goal may be to improve productivity by 20% within the next 6 months.

Step 3: Develop a well-defined strategy

The third step is to develop a well-defined strategy for achieving the goal. The strategy should be based on the strengths and weaknesses of the business and should be aligned with the overall business strategy. For example, if the business is experiencing financial distress, the strategy may involve reducing costs, increasing revenue, or restructuring debt. If the business is experiencing operational inefficiencies, the strategy may involve improving processes, increasing automation, or reorganizing the workforce.

Step 4: Develop a detailed action plan

The fourth step is to develop a detailed action plan for implementing the strategy. The action plan should include specific steps, timelines, and responsibilities. Each step should be broken down into smaller, manageable tasks that can be easily monitored and measured. The action plan should also identify the resources required, such as funding, personnel, or technology.

For example, if the strategy involves reducing costs, the action plan may include tasks such as negotiating with suppliers, streamlining processes, or reducing headcount. Each task should have a clear timeline and responsibility assigned to it.

Step 5: Implement the action plan

The fifth step is to implement the action plan. This involves putting the plan into action and monitoring progress. Each task should be closely monitored and evaluated to ensure that it is on track and aligned with the overall strategy. Regular progress reports should be produced and shared with all stakeholders to ensure transparency and accountability.

Step 6: Monitor and evaluate progress

The final step is to monitor and evaluate progress. This involves tracking the KPIs identified in the monitoring and evaluation framework and making necessary adjustments. Regular progress reports should be produced and shared with all stakeholders to ensure transparency and accountability. The monitoring and evaluation framework should also include a feedback loop to allow for continuous improvement and learning.

Examples of Comprehensive Turnaround Plans

Example 1: Ford Motor Company

In the mid-2000s, Ford Motor Company was facing significant financial distress. The company had been losing market share to its competitors, and its financial performance had been declining for several years. In response, Ford developed a comprehensive turnaround plan that involved several key elements:

1. Diagnosis of the problem: Ford identified several root causes of the problem, including high costs, declining sales, and low profitability.
2. Assessment of the current state: Ford conducted a thorough analysis of its financial and

operational performance and identified areas that required improvement.

3. Clear and measurable goal: Ford set a clear and measurable goal to achieve profitability by 2009.
4. Well-defined strategy: Ford developed a well-defined strategy that involved reducing costs, increasing revenue, and investing in new products.
5. Detailed action plan: Ford developed a detailed action plan that included specific steps, timelines, and responsibilities. The plan included reducing headcount, negotiating with suppliers, and investing in new products.
6. Monitoring and evaluation framework: Ford developed a monitoring and evaluation framework to track progress and make necessary adjustments. The framework included KPIs such as profitability, market share, and cash flow.

As a result of this comprehensive turnaround plan, Ford was able to achieve profitability by 2009 and has since become a leading player in the automotive industry.

Example 2: Starbucks Corporation

In the early 2000s, Starbucks Corporation was facing declining sales and operational inefficiencies. The company had grown rapidly in the previous decade, but its growth had slowed, and its brand had become diluted.

In response, Starbucks developed a comprehensive turnaround plan that involved several key elements:

1. Diagnosis of the problem: Starbucks identified several root causes of the problem, including declining sales, operational inefficiencies, and a diluted brand.
2. Assessment of the current state: Starbucks conducted a thorough analysis of its financial and operational performance and identified areas that required improvement.
3. Clear and measurable goal: Starbucks set a clear and measurable goal to reinvigorate the brand and improve operational efficiency.
4. Well-defined strategy: Starbucks developed a well-defined strategy that involved retraining employees, improving store layouts, and streamlining operations.
5. Detailed action plan: Starbucks developed a detailed action plan that included specific steps, timelines, and responsibilities. The plan included retraining employees, improving store layouts, and streamlining operations.
6. Monitoring and evaluation framework: Starbucks developed a monitoring and evaluation framework to track progress and make necessary adjustments. The framework included

KPIs such as same-store sales growth, customer satisfaction, and store efficiency.

As a result of this comprehensive turnaround plan, Starbucks was able to reinvigorate its brand and improve operational efficiency. The company has since regained its position as a leader in the coffee industry and has continued to grow and innovate.

Example 3: General Electric Company

In the late 2010s, General Electric Company was facing significant financial and operational challenges. The company had been struggling to maintain profitability, and its stock price had been declining for several years. In response, General Electric developed a comprehensive turnaround plan that involved several key elements:

1. Diagnosis of the problem: General Electric identified several root causes of the problem, including high costs, declining revenue, and a lack of focus.
2. Assessment of the current state: General Electric conducted a thorough analysis of its financial and operational performance and identified areas that required improvement.
3. Clear and measurable goal: General Electric set a clear and measurable goal to improve profitability and refocus the business on core areas.
4. Well-defined strategy: General Electric developed a well-defined strategy that involved reducing costs, divesting non-core businesses, and focusing on key growth areas.

5. Detailed action plan: General Electric developed a detailed action plan that included specific steps, timelines, and responsibilities. The plan included reducing headcount, divesting non-core businesses, and investing in key growth areas such as renewable energy and healthcare.
6. Monitoring and evaluation framework: General Electric developed a monitoring and evaluation framework to track progress and make necessary adjustments. The framework included KPIs such as profitability, revenue growth, and return on investment.

As a result of this comprehensive turnaround plan, General Electric has been able to improve its financial performance and refocus the business on core areas. While the company still faces challenges, it has made significant progress in turning around its fortunes.

In conclusion, developing and implementing a comprehensive turnaround plan can be a complex and challenging process, but it is essential for organizations facing financial or operational distress. By following the six steps outlined in this essay, organizations can develop a clear and effective plan for turning around their fortunes. The key is to diagnose the problem, assess the current state, set clear goals, develop a well-defined strategy, create a detailed action plan, and monitor and evaluate progress. The examples of Ford Motor Company, Starbucks Corporation, and General Electric Company illustrate how these steps can be applied in practice to achieve successful turnarounds.

Chapter 3

Conduct a Market Analysis

To be successful in turning around a distressed hotel, it is important to have a good understanding of the market in which the property is located. This includes an analysis of the competition, current market conditions, and trends.

Example: The Westin Peachtree Plaza in Atlanta suffered from declining occupancy rates due to increased competition from other hotels in the area. The owner conducted a market analysis and identified several ways to differentiate the hotel from its competitors, such as offering unique amenities and services. As a result, the hotel was able to increase its occupancy rates.

In today's world, the hospitality industry has become one of the most competitive and dynamic industries. The COVID-19 pandemic has greatly impacted this industry, and many hotels have been left struggling to remain afloat. The key to surviving in such an environment is to conduct a comprehensive market analysis and use the data obtained to facilitate a viable business plan. In this chapter, we will discuss the key steps involved in conducting a market analysis, using data to facilitate a business plan, and provide examples of each statement.

Step 1: Conducting a Market Analysis

Conducting a market analysis is an essential first step in any business plan. It involves researching the current market trends, assessing the competition, and identifying the target market. The following are the key steps involved in conducting a market analysis.

1.1 Researching Current Market Trends

The first step in conducting a market analysis is to research the current market trends. This involves collecting and analyzing data on the current state of the hospitality industry, including industry trends, customer preferences, and market size. This information can be obtained from industry publications, market research reports, and government statistics.

For example, according to a recent report by ResearchAndMarkets.com, the global hotel industry was valued at USD 589.18 billion in 2020, with a projected growth rate of 10.4% from 2021 to 2028. This data provides an insight into the current state of the hotel industry and the potential growth opportunities available.

1.2 Assessing the Competition

Assessing the competition is another crucial step in conducting a market analysis. It involves researching and analyzing the strengths and weaknesses of direct and indirect competitors. This can help the business identify areas where it can differentiate itself from its competitors and gain a competitive advantage.

For example, a distressed hotel may have to conduct a competitive analysis to determine its unique selling points. One way to do this is by analyzing customer reviews of the hotel and its competitors. This data can be obtained from various online review platforms such as TripAdvisor, Yelp, and Google Reviews. By analyzing these reviews, the hotel can identify areas where it needs to improve and areas where it is performing well.

1.3 Identifying the Target Market

The final step in conducting a market analysis is to identify the target market. This involves analyzing demographic data, such as age, income, and location, to determine the customer segment that is most likely to use the hotel's services. By identifying the target market, the hotel can develop marketing strategies and promotions that are tailored to the needs and preferences of its target audience.

For example, a hotel may identify that its target market is business travelers who require a quiet and comfortable environment to work. In this case, the hotel can offer amenities such as high-speed internet, comfortable workspaces, and a quiet environment to attract this segment of customers.

Step 2: Using Data to Facilitate a Business Plan

Once the market analysis is complete, the next step is to use the data obtained to facilitate a business plan. The following are the key steps involved in using data to facilitate a business plan.

2.1 Developing a SWOT Analysis

The first step in using data to facilitate a business plan is to develop a SWOT analysis. This involves analyzing the strengths, weaknesses, opportunities, and threats of the business. By analyzing the data obtained from the market analysis, the business can identify its strengths and weaknesses, as well as the opportunities and threats in the market.

For example, a distressed hotel may identify its strengths as its location, brand reputation, and quality of service. Its weaknesses may include outdated facilities and a lack of amenities. The opportunities in the market may include a growing demand for luxury hotels, while the threats may include competition from newer hotels in the area.

2.2 Defining the Business Objectives

The next step in using data to facilitate a business plan is to define the business objectives. This involves setting specific, measurable, achievable, relevant, and time-bound (SMART) goals for the business. The business objectives should be based on the SWOT analysis and the data obtained from the market analysis.

For example, a distressed hotel may set a SMART goal to increase its occupancy rate by 10% in the next 6 months by targeting business travelers and offering attractive promotional packages.

2.3 Developing a Marketing Strategy

The third step in using data to facilitate a business plan is to develop a marketing strategy. This involves developing a plan to promote the hotel's services to its target market. The marketing strategy should be based on the data obtained from the market analysis and should be aligned with the business objectives.

For example, a distressed hotel may develop a marketing strategy that focuses on promoting its newly renovated rooms and amenities to business travelers. The hotel can offer special promotional packages, such as discounted rates for extended stays or free Wi-Fi, to attract this segment of customers. The hotel can also use targeted online advertising and email marketing to reach its target audience.

2.4 Creating Financial Projections

The final step in using data to facilitate a business plan is to create financial projections. This involves projecting the expected revenues and expenses of the business based on the data obtained from the market analysis and the business objectives. Financial projections can help the business determine the feasibility of its business plan and identify areas where it may need to make adjustments.

For example, a distressed hotel may project its revenues based on the expected occupancy rate, average room rate, and other revenue streams such as food and beverage sales. The hotel can also project its expenses, such as labor costs, utilities, and marketing expenses. By comparing the projected revenues and expenses, the hotel can determine its profitability and make adjustments to its business plan as needed.

Conducting a comprehensive market analysis and using the data obtained to facilitate a business plan is crucial for the success of any business, especially in a competitive and dynamic industry like hospitality. By researching the current market trends, assessing the competition, and identifying the target market, a business can develop a SWOT analysis and define its business objectives. The business can then develop a marketing strategy and create financial projections based on the data obtained.

In conclusion, for a distressed hotel, conducting a market analysis can provide valuable insights into the current state of the industry and help identify areas where the hotel can differentiate itself from its competitors. By using the data obtained to facilitate a business plan, the hotel can set SMART goals, develop a marketing strategy, and create financial projections that can help it survive and thrive in a challenging environment.

Chapter 4

Identify the Target Market

It is important to identify the target market for the hotel in order to develop a marketing strategy that will resonate with potential guests. The target market may be different than what was originally intended, and adjustments may need to be made to the hotel's amenities and services to meet the needs of the target market.

Example: The St. Regis in San Francisco struggled with low occupancy rates due to an outdated image. The owner conducted a market analysis and identified a new target market for the hotel - the tech industry. The hotel was renovated to meet the needs of this target market, including the addition of high-tech amenities, and was able to increase occupancy rates.

In the hospitality industry, identifying the target market for a hotel is crucial for success. It helps in determining the type of guests that are most likely to stay at the hotel and cater to their needs. A hotel's target market can be identified through various methods, such as analyzing demographic data, studying travel trends, and conducting market research. This chapter will discuss how to identify a hotel's target market and use data to facilitate a business plan for a distressed hotel, along with examples of each statement.

Section 1: Identifying the Target Market

1.1 Analyzing Demographic Data

One way to identify a hotel's target market is by analyzing demographic data. Demographic data includes information such as age, gender, income level, education level, and marital status. Analyzing this data can help a hotel understand the type of guests that are most likely to stay at the hotel. For example, if a hotel is located near a university, it may cater to students and their families. On the other hand, if a hotel is located near a business district, it may cater to business travelers.

Example: The James Hotel in Chicago

The James Hotel in Chicago is a luxury boutique hotel that caters to young professionals and affluent travelers. The hotel is located in the River North neighborhood, which is known for its art galleries, restaurants, and nightlife. The hotel's target market is primarily young professionals who enjoy staying in trendy and upscale accommodations. The hotel's rooms feature modern decor and high-end amenities, such as Nespresso machines and rain showers. The hotel also offers a rooftop bar with views of the city skyline, which is a popular spot for young professionals to socialize after work.

1.2 Studying Travel Trends

Another way to identify a hotel's target market is by studying travel trends. Travel trends include factors such as travel purpose, seasonality, and destination preferences. Understanding travel trends can help a hotel determine the type of guests that are most likely to stay at the hotel and cater to their needs. For example, if a hotel is located in a popular beach destination, it may cater to leisure travelers looking for a relaxing vacation.

Example: The Standard Hotel in Miami

The Standard Hotel in Miami is a trendy hotel that caters to young, stylish travelers. The hotel is located on Belle Isle, a small island in Biscayne Bay, and is known for its minimalist design and unique amenities. The hotel's target market is primarily young, hip travelers who are interested in fashion, art, and nightlife. The hotel offers a variety of amenities, such as a rooftop spa, yoga classes, and a clothing-optional pool. These amenities are designed to attract young, adventurous travelers who are looking for a unique and exciting vacation experience.

1.3 Conducting Market Research

Finally, another way to identify a hotel's target market is by conducting market research. Market research involves gathering data from potential customers to understand their preferences, needs, and behaviors. This information can help a hotel determine the type of guests that are most likely to stay at the hotel and cater to their needs. For example, if a hotel is planning to launch a new restaurant, it may conduct market research to determine the type of cuisine that is most popular among its target market.

Example: The Ace Hotel in New York City

The Ace Hotel in New York City is a trendy boutique hotel that caters to creative and artistic travelers. The hotel is located in the Flatiron District, a neighborhood known for its design and architecture. The hotel's target market is primarily young, creative professionals who are interested in art, design, and culture. The hotel offers a variety of amenities, such as a gallery space, a bookstore, and a co-working space. These amenities are designed to attract creative professionals who are looking for a hotel that reflects their interests and values.

Section 2: Facilitating a Business Plan for a Distressed Hotel Using Data

Once a hotel has identified its target market, it can use this information to facilitate a business plan for a distressed hotel. A distressed hotel is one that is struggling financially and may be in danger of closing. By using data to identify the target market, a hotel can develop a business plan that caters to the needs and preferences of its most likely guests.

2.1 Conducting a SWOT Analysis

Before developing a business plan, a distressed hotel should conduct a SWOT analysis. A SWOT analysis is an assessment of the hotel's strengths, weaknesses, opportunities, and threats. By analyzing these factors, a hotel can determine its current position in the market and develop a strategy to improve its financial performance.

Example: The Palmer House Hilton in Chicago

The Palmer House Hilton in Chicago is a historic hotel that was struggling financially due to increasing competition from newer hotels in the area. To develop a business plan, the hotel conducted a SWOT analysis. The hotel's strengths included its prime location in downtown Chicago and its reputation as a historic landmark. The hotel's weaknesses included outdated decor and amenities that did not appeal to younger travelers. The hotel's opportunities included its potential to attract business travelers and its prime location near popular tourist attractions. The hotel's threats included increasing competition from newer hotels and changing consumer preferences.

2.2 Developing a Marketing Strategy

Once a SWOT analysis has been conducted, a distressed hotel should develop a marketing strategy that targets its identified target market. The marketing strategy should include tactics such as social media marketing, email marketing, and targeted advertising. By developing a marketing strategy that caters to the needs and preferences of its target market, a hotel can increase its visibility and attract more guests.

Example: The St. Regis Hotel in New York City

The St. Regis Hotel in New York City is a luxury hotel that was struggling financially due to increased competition from other luxury hotels in the area. To develop a marketing strategy, the hotel identified its target market as affluent travelers who value luxury and exclusivity. The hotel developed a social media marketing campaign that showcased its high-end amenities, such as a butler service and a private rooftop terrace. The hotel also developed targeted advertising campaigns that were placed in luxury lifestyle magazines and online publications. As a result of these efforts, the hotel was able to increase its occupancy rate and improve its financial performance.

2.3 Upgrading Amenities and Services

To appeal to its target market, a distressed hotel should upgrade its amenities and services. By offering high-end amenities and services, a hotel can attract guests who are willing to pay a premium for luxury and exclusivity. Some examples of amenities and services that can be upgraded include room decor, in-room technology, and food and beverage offerings.

Example: The Waldorf Astoria in Beverly Hills

The Waldorf Astoria in Beverly Hills is a luxury hotel that was struggling financially due to its outdated decor and amenities. To appeal to its target market of affluent travelers who value luxury and exclusivity, the hotel upgraded its amenities and services. The hotel renovated its guest rooms to feature modern decor and high-end amenities such as Frette linens, Nespresso machines, and marble bathrooms. The hotel also added new food and beverage offerings, including a rooftop bar and restaurant that offers panoramic views of the city. As a result of these upgrades, the hotel was able to attract more guests and increase its revenue.

Identifying a hotel's target market is crucial for success in the hospitality industry. It helps in determining the type of guests that are most likely to stay at the hotel and cater to their needs. By using data to identify the target market, a distressed hotel can develop a business plan that caters to the needs and preferences of its most likely guests. Conducting a SWOT analysis, developing a marketing strategy, and upgrading amenities and services are all important steps in this process.

It's also important to note that a hotel's target market may evolve over time due to changes in consumer preferences or shifts in the market. Therefore, it's essential for hotels to regularly analyze their target market and adjust their strategies accordingly.

In conclusion, identifying a hotel's target market is essential for developing a successful business plan, especially for distressed hotels. By understanding the needs and preferences of its most likely guests and catering to them, a hotel can increase its occupancy rates and improve its financial performance. Through careful analysis of market data and strategic planning, a distressed hotel can turn its fortunes around and thrive in a highly competitive industry.

Chapter 5

Invest in Renovations

Renovations can help to refresh the property's image and make it more appealing to guests. This can include upgrades to guest rooms, public spaces, and amenities.

Example: The Hotel Crescent Court in Dallas was suffering from low occupancy rates due to outdated guest rooms and public spaces. The owner invested in a comprehensive renovation that included the addition of new amenities, such as a spa and fitness center, and upgraded guest rooms. As a result, the hotel was able to increase its occupancy rates.

Investing in hotel renovations is a crucial aspect

of managing a successful hotel business. A distressed hotel requires special attention to ensure that its condition is improved to attract more customers and increase profitability. The renovation process involves a combination of upgrading facilities, remodeling rooms, and improving the hotel's overall appearance. In this chapter, I will discuss the steps required to invest in hotel renovations for a distressed hotel using examples of successful hotel renovations.

Step 1: Evaluate the current condition of the hotel

Before embarking on any renovation project, it is essential to evaluate the current condition of the hotel. This evaluation should include assessing the physical condition of the hotel, analyzing customer feedback, and evaluating the competition. The physical condition of the hotel involves examining the facilities, equipment, and infrastructure to identify any deficiencies or areas that require improvement. Customer feedback can be collected through surveys, reviews, and social media platforms to identify areas that customers feel need improvement. The competition analysis involves assessing the features and amenities offered by other hotels in the area to determine areas of improvement.

For example, the Hotel Figueroa in Los Angeles was a distressed hotel that underwent a $60 million renovation. The renovation included upgrading the facilities, remodeling rooms, and enhancing the hotel's overall appearance. Before embarking on the renovation project, the hotel's management conducted a comprehensive evaluation of the hotel's physical condition, analyzed customer feedback, and evaluated the competition. This evaluation helped the management to identify areas that required improvement, and as a result, the renovation project was a success.

Step 2: Set a budget and timeline for the renovation project

Once the hotel's current condition has been evaluated, the next step is to set a budget and timeline for the renovation project. The budget should be realistic and consider all the expenses involved in the renovation project, including labor costs, materials, permits, and taxes. The timeline should also be realistic and consider the time required to complete the renovation project without disrupting the hotel's operations.

For example, the Plaza Hotel in New York City underwent a $450 million renovation that took three years to complete. The renovation project involved upgrading facilities, remodeling rooms, and enhancing the hotel's overall appearance. The management set a realistic budget and timeline for the renovation project, and as a result, the project was completed without any major disruptions to the hotel's operations.

Step 3: Prioritize areas of improvement

Not all areas of a hotel require the same level of improvement. It is essential to prioritize areas of improvement based on their impact on the hotel's overall appearance, customer experience, and profitability. Areas that have a significant impact on customer experience and profitability should be prioritized over areas that have a minimal impact.

For example, the Marriott Marquis in Washington, D.C., underwent a $30 million renovation that focused on improving the hotel's lobby and public spaces. The renovation project involved upgrading the hotel's restaurants, bars, and meeting spaces to enhance customer experience and profitability. The management prioritized these areas of improvement over room renovations because they had a more significant impact on the hotel's overall appearance and customer experience.

Step 4: Hire a reputable contractor

The success of any renovation project depends on the contractor's quality of work. It is essential to hire a reputable contractor who has experience in hotel renovations. The contractor should be licensed, insured, and have a track record of successfully completing hotel renovation projects.

For example, the Hotel Del Coronado in San Diego underwent a $200 million renovation that involved upgrading facilities, remodeling rooms, and enhancing the hotel's overall appearance. The hotel's management hired a reputable contractor who had experience in hotel renovations, and as a result, the renovation project was completed on time and within budget.

Step 5: Communicate with customers

During the renovation process, it is essential to communicate with customers to manage their expectations and minimize the impact of the renovation project on their experience. Communication can be done through various channels, including social media platforms, email newsletters, and in-person meetings. Customers should be informed of any disruptions that may occur during the renovation project, such as noise or temporary closures of facilities.

For example, the Hotel Emma in San Antonio underwent a $100 million renovation that involved upgrading facilities, remodeling rooms, and enhancing the hotel's overall appearance. The hotel's management communicated with customers through various channels, including social media, email newsletters, and in-person meetings. Customers were informed of the renovation project's timeline and any disruptions that may occur, and as a result, the renovation project was completed without any major issues.

Step 6: Monitor the renovation project

During the renovation process, it is essential to monitor the progress of the project to ensure that it is completed on time and within budget. Regular inspections should be conducted to ensure that the work is being done to the required quality standards. Any issues or delays should be addressed promptly to avoid any major disruptions to the project timeline.

For example, the Fairmont Royal York in Toronto underwent a $110 million renovation that involved upgrading facilities, remodeling rooms, and enhancing the hotel's overall appearance. The hotel's management monitored the renovation project closely and conducted regular inspections to ensure that the work was being done to the required quality standards. Any issues or delays were addressed promptly, and as a result, the renovation project was completed on time and within budget.

Step 7: Evaluate the impact of the renovation project

After the renovation project is completed, it is essential to evaluate its impact on the hotel's operations, customer experience, and profitability. This evaluation should involve analyzing customer feedback, comparing financial performance before and after the renovation project, and assessing the hotel's competitiveness in the market.

For example, the Waldorf Astoria in New York City underwent a $1 billion renovation that involved upgrading facilities, remodeling rooms, and enhancing the hotel's overall appearance. The renovation project was completed in 2021, and the hotel's management evaluated its impact on the hotel's operations, customer experience, and profitability. The evaluation showed that the renovation project had a significant positive impact on the hotel's financial performance, customer satisfaction, and competitiveness in the market.

In conclusion, investing in hotel renovations is a crucial aspect of managing a successful hotel business. A distressed hotel requires special attention to ensure that its condition is improved to attract more customers and increase profitability. The renovation process involves a combination of upgrading facilities, remodeling rooms, and improving the hotel's overall appearance. To invest in hotel renovations for a distressed hotel successfully, it is essential to evaluate the current condition of the hotel, set a budget and timeline for the renovation project, prioritize areas of improvement, hire a reputable contractor, communicate with customers, monitor the renovation project, and evaluate its impact. By following these steps and using examples of successful hotel renovations, hotel managers can transform a distressed hotel into a thriving business.

Chapter 6

Train Staff

Customer service is a key factor in the success of a hotel. By investing in staff training, hotel owners can ensure that their employees provide high-quality service to guests, which can lead to positive reviews and repeat business.

Example: The Four Seasons in New York City struggled with poor customer service, which was impacting its occupancy rates. The owner invested in staff training to improve the quality of service provided by employees. As a result, the hotel's reputation improved, and occupancy rates increased.

The hospitality industry is constantly evolving and requires regular staff training to maintain the high standards expected by guests. However, in some cases, hotels may experience periods of distress due to various factors such as economic downturns, natural disasters, or changes in the competitive landscape. During these times, staff training becomes even more critical, as it can help hotels navigate the challenges and emerge stronger. In this chapter, we will discuss how to conduct staff training for a distressed hotel using examples of each statement.

Assess the Current Situation

The first step in conducting staff training for a

distressed hotel is to assess the current situation. This includes evaluating the hotel's financial position, occupancy rates, customer satisfaction scores, and employee morale. By understanding the hotel's current state, managers can identify areas of improvement and tailor the training program to meet specific needs.

For example, let's consider a hotel that has experienced a significant decline in occupancy rates due to increased competition in the area. The hotel management team conducts a survey of guests to identify areas where the hotel is falling short. They find that guests are dissatisfied with the cleanliness of the rooms, the quality of the food, and the level of service provided by staff.

Based on this information, the hotel management team can develop a training program that focuses on improving room cleanliness, food quality, and customer service skills. The program may include sessions on proper cleaning techniques, food preparation, and communication skills, among other topics.

Set Clear Goals

Once the current situation has been assessed, the next step is to set clear goals for the training program. Goals should be specific, measurable, achievable, relevant, and time-bound (SMART). This ensures that the training program is effective and that progress can be tracked and evaluated.

For example, let's consider a hotel that is experiencing a decline in customer satisfaction scores due to poor service. The hotel management team sets a goal to improve customer satisfaction scores by 10% within six months. To achieve this goal, they develop a training program that focuses on improving customer service skills, such as communication, problem-solving, and conflict resolution.

The training program includes sessions on active listening, empathy, and handling difficult customers. The hotel management team tracks customer satisfaction scores over the next six months and finds that they have improved by 12%, exceeding their goal.

Develop Engaging Content

The success of a training program depends on the quality of the content. To ensure that the training program is effective, managers must develop engaging content that is relevant and practical. The content should be tailored to the needs of the staff and should be delivered in a format that is easy to understand.

For example, let's consider a hotel that is experiencing a decline in revenue due to low sales in the restaurant. The hotel management team develops a training program that focuses on improving the quality of the food and the level of service provided by the restaurant staff.

The training program includes sessions on food

preparation, presentation, and customer service. To make the content more engaging, the hotel management team includes hands-on activities, such as food tasting sessions and role-playing exercises.

Use a Variety of Training Methods

To ensure that staff training is effective, managers must use a variety of training methods. This ensures that staff members are engaged and can learn in a way that suits their learning style. Training methods can include classroom-style lectures, hands-on activities, e-learning modules, and on-the-job training.

For example, let's consider a hotel that is experiencing a decline in occupancy rates due to poor online reviews. The hotel management team develops a training program that focuses on improving the hotel's online presence and reputation.

The training program includes sessions on social media management, online review management, and search engine optimization. To make the training more effective, the hotel management team also includes on-the-job training sessions where staff members are paired with experienced colleagues who can provide feedback and support as they navigate online platforms.

Provide Ongoing Support and Feedback

To ensure that staff training is effective, managers must provide ongoing support and feedback.

This includes regular check-ins with staff members to evaluate progress, provide additional training as needed, and recognize achievements. By providing ongoing support, staff members feel valued and motivated to continue learning and improving.

For example, let's consider a hotel that is experiencing a decline in employee morale due to recent layoffs. The hotel management team develops a training program that focuses on improving employee morale by providing support and recognition.

The training program includes sessions on effective communication, team-building, and recognition strategies. To provide ongoing support, the hotel management team schedules regular check-ins with staff members to evaluate progress and provide additional training as needed. They also implement an employee recognition program that rewards staff members for their hard work and achievements.

Evaluate the Effectiveness of the Training Program

The final step in conducting staff training for a distressed hotel is to evaluate the effectiveness of the training program. This includes measuring the impact of the training program on key performance indicators such as customer satisfaction, occupancy rates, and employee morale.

By evaluating the effectiveness of the training program, managers can identify areas of improvement and make adjustments as needed to ensure continued success.

For example, let's consider a hotel that has implemented a training program focused on improving customer service skills. The hotel management team evaluates the effectiveness of the program by measuring customer satisfaction scores before and after the training program.

They find that customer satisfaction scores have improved by 15%, indicating that the training program has been successful. Based on this evaluation, the hotel management team decides to continue the training program and incorporate additional modules to further improve customer service skills.

In conclusion, conducting staff training for a distressed hotel is crucial to navigate through challenging times and emerge stronger. By assessing the current situation, setting clear goals, developing engaging content, using a variety of training methods, providing ongoing support and feedback, and evaluating the effectiveness of the training program, managers can ensure that staff members are equipped with the skills and knowledge needed to provide excellent service and drive success.

The examples provided in this chapter illustrate how staff training can be tailored to specific needs and challenges, such as improving customer service, increasing revenue, and boosting employee morale. By implementing these strategies, hotels can overcome the challenges of distress and thrive in a competitive hospitality industry.

Chapter 7

Offer Unique Amenities and Services

To stand out in a competitive market, it is important for hotels to offer unique amenities and services that are not available at other properties. This can help to attract guests and increase occupancy rates.

Example: The NoMad Hotel in New York City offers a unique library and lounge that includes a large collection of books and a cozy fireplace. This amenity helps the hotel to stand out from other properties in the area and has contributed to its success.

The hotel industry is a highly competitive one, with new hotels and resorts opening up every day, all offering unique amenities and services to attract guests. In this dynamic landscape, distressed hotels face an even greater challenge, as they must find a way to differentiate themselves from their competition while trying to overcome financial difficulties. In this chapter, we will explore the various ways in which distressed hotels can offer unique services and amenities to their guests, with examples of each statement.

Focus on the guest experience

Distressed hotels should focus on delivering an exceptional guest experience that is personalized, memorable, and exceeds expectations. This can be achieved by offering personalized welcome amenities, such as a welcome drink or snack, a personalized note or card in the room, or a personalized greeting from staff members. Personalized services, such as concierge services, can also enhance the guest experience.

The W Chicago City Center is an example of a distressed hotel that offers personalized services and amenities to its guests. The hotel offers a "Whatever/Whenever" service that allows guests to customize their experience by requesting anything they desire, from a custom-made cocktail to a romantic evening for two.

Offer unique and innovative dining options

Distressed hotels can offer unique and innovative dining options to attract guests. This can include partnerships with local restaurants or chefs, offering themed dining experiences, or creating signature dishes that are only available at the hotel.

The Ritz-Carlton, Amelia Island is an example of a distressed hotel that offers unique and innovative dining options. The hotel has partnered with renowned chef Michael Voltaggio to create a restaurant that offers a culinary journey through the coastal South. The restaurant also features an interactive kitchen where guests can watch the chefs at work.

Create a sense of community

Distressed hotels can create a sense of community by offering shared spaces where guests can interact and engage with each other. This can include communal dining areas, shared workspaces, or common lounges.

The Ace Hotel in New York City is an example of a distressed hotel that creates a sense of community. The hotel features a communal lobby that serves as a gathering place for guests and locals alike. The lobby features a bar, lounge areas, and a coffee shop, and hosts a variety of events, including live music, poetry readings, and art exhibits.

Emphasize wellness and self-care

Distressed hotels can emphasize wellness and self-care by offering amenities such as fitness centers, spa services, and wellness programs. This can include yoga classes, meditation sessions, or healthy food options.

The Four Seasons Resort Maui at Wailea is an example of a distressed hotel that emphasizes wellness and self-care. The hotel offers a variety of wellness programs, including a "wellness your way" package that allows guests to customize their wellness experience. The hotel also features a state-of-the-art fitness center and a world-class spa.

Provide unique entertainment options

Distressed hotels can provide unique entertainment options to attract guests. This can include partnerships with local entertainment venues or artists, offering themed entertainment experiences, or creating signature events that are only available at the hotel.

The W Hollywood is an example of a distressed hotel that provides unique entertainment options. The hotel features a rooftop pool and bar that hosts a variety of events, including pool parties and live music performances. The hotel also partners with local entertainment venues to offer guests exclusive access to concerts and shows.

Embrace sustainability

Distressed hotels can embrace sustainability by implementing environmentally friendly practices and offering eco-friendly amenities. This can include using renewable energy sources, reducing waste, and offering sustainable food options.

The 1 Hotel South Beach is an example of a distressed hotel that embraces sustainability. The hotel is powered by renewable energy and features eco-friendly materials throughout the property. The hotel also offers sustainable food options, with a focus on locally sourced and organic ingredients.

Offer unique outdoor experiences

Distressed hotels can offer unique outdoor experiences to attract guests. This can include partnerships with local adventure companies or offering unique outdoor activities on the property.

The Chateau Montelena Winery in Napa Valley is an example of a distressed hotel that offers unique outdoor experiences. The hotel features a vineyard and winery, as well as a variety of outdoor activities, such as hiking, biking, and hot air balloon rides.

Provide exceptional customer service

Distressed hotels can provide exceptional customer service to differentiate themselves from their competition. This can include training staff to anticipate guest needs and providing personalized attention to each guest.

The St. Regis Bali Resort is an example of a distressed hotel that provides exceptional customer service. The hotel offers a personal butler service to each guest, who is available 24/7 to cater to their needs. The butler service includes a range of personalized services, such as unpacking luggage, drawing a bath, or arranging local tours.

Incorporate local culture

Distressed hotels can incorporate local culture into their services and amenities to provide guests with a unique and authentic experience. This can include partnering with local artisans or offering cultural experiences, such as cooking classes or guided tours.

The Andaz Amsterdam Prinsengracht is an example of a distressed hotel that incorporates local culture into its services and amenities. The hotel features an art collection that showcases local artists and offers guests a chance to learn about Dutch culture through their stay. The hotel also partners with local chefs to offer unique dining experiences that incorporate local ingredients and flavors.

In conclusion, distressed hotels can offer unique services and amenities to differentiate themselves from their competition and attract guests. By focusing on the guest experience, offering unique and innovative dining options, creating a sense of community, emphasizing wellness and self-care, providing unique entertainment options, embracing sustainability, offering unique outdoor experiences, providing exceptional customer service, and incorporating local culture, distressed hotels can create a unique and memorable experience for their guests. These strategies can help to increase occupancy rates and revenue, as well as improve the hotel's overall financial performance.

Chapter 8

Increase Marketing Efforts

Marketing is a critical component of a successful hotel turnaround. By increasing marketing efforts, hotel owners can increase brand awareness and attract new guests.

Example: The Marriott Marquis in New York City was struggling with low occupancy rates due to increased competition from new hotels in the area. The owner increased the hotel's marketing efforts, including digital advertising and social media campaigns. As a result, the hotel was able to attract more guests and increase occupancy rates.

The hospitality industry has been hit hard by the COVID-19 pandemic, and many hotels are facing financial distress. However, with effective marketing efforts, it is possible to increase the hotel's visibility, attract more guests, and boost revenue. This chapter will discuss how to increase marketing efforts for a distressed hotel using various examples to illustrate each statement.

Conduct Market Research

Before developing a marketing strategy, it is essential to conduct market research to understand the hotel's current position, its target audience, and the competition. This research will help identify the hotel's strengths, weaknesses, opportunities, and threats

(SWOT analysis), which can be used to develop a successful marketing plan.

For example, the Four Seasons Hotel in New York conducted market research to identify the reasons why guests were choosing other hotels over theirs. They discovered that many guests were leaving the hotel because of the high cost of food and drinks. As a result, the hotel decided to lower the prices of their food and drinks, which led to an increase in guest satisfaction and revenue.

Similarly, a distressed hotel could conduct market research to identify the reasons why guests are not choosing their hotel. They could conduct surveys to gather feedback from guests and analyze online reviews to understand the hotel's strengths and weaknesses.

Develop a Unique Value Proposition

A unique value proposition (UVP) is a statement that explains why guests should choose a particular hotel over its competitors. Developing a UVP is critical in the hospitality industry, where hotels are offering similar services and amenities.

For example, the Ace Hotel in New York has a unique value proposition that appeals to millennial guests. Their UVP is "Experience the city like a local," which emphasizes their focus on local culture and authenticity. They offer guests a personalized experience by providing locally sourced products, free Wi-Fi, and curated local events.

A distressed hotel could develop a UVP that emphasizes its unique selling points. For example, if the hotel is located near a tourist attraction, its UVP could be "Stay at the closest hotel to [tourist attraction]," or if the hotel has a spa, its UVP could be "Relax and rejuvenate at our award-winning spa."

Use Digital Marketing Strategies

Digital marketing has become essential for hotels to reach a broader audience and increase bookings. Digital marketing includes strategies such as search engine optimization (SEO), social media marketing, email marketing, and online advertising.

For example, The Ritz-Carlton Hotels use social media marketing to showcase their luxury amenities and services to a global audience. Their Instagram account has over 1 million followers, and they regularly post photos and videos of their hotels' stunning views, exquisite cuisine, and relaxing spas.

A distressed hotel could use digital marketing strategies to increase its online visibility. They could optimize their website for search engines, create social media accounts to engage with guests, and use email marketing to promote their hotel to previous guests.

Offer Packages and Special Deals

Offering packages and special deals is an effective way to attract guests and increase revenue. Hotels can offer packages that include accommodation, meals, and activities, or special deals that offer discounts or added value.

For example, The Ritz-Carlton Hotel in Bali offers a "Stay 3 Nights, Pay for 2" promotion, which provides guests with a free night's stay when they book a three-night stay. This promotion encourages guests to stay longer, which increases revenue for the hotel.

A distressed hotel could offer packages or special deals to attract more guests. For example, they could offer a package that includes accommodation and meals, or offer discounts for longer stays. They could also offer promotions during off-peak seasons to increase occupancy.

Use Influencer Marketing

Influencer marketing is a powerful tool for hotels to increase their visibility and attract new guests. Influencers are individuals who have a large social media following and can promote the hotel to their followers.

For example, The Cosmopolitan Hotel in Las Vegas partnered with popular influencers to promote their hotel to a younger audience. The influencers created content that showcased the hotel's amenities, nightlife, and restaurants, which appealed to their followers.

A distressed hotel could use influencer marketing to reach a wider audience. They could partner with local influencers or social media personalities who have a similar target audience to their hotel. The influencers could create content that highlights the hotel's unique features and promote special deals or packages.

Provide Exceptional Customer Service

Exceptional customer service is essential in the hospitality industry and can be a powerful marketing tool. Guests who receive excellent service are more likely to return to the hotel and recommend it to others.

For example, The Peninsula Hotel in Chicago has a reputation for exceptional customer service. They have a team of staff who provide personalized service to each guest, from remembering their names to anticipating their needs.

A distressed hotel could focus on providing exceptional customer service to improve guest satisfaction and encourage repeat business. They could train their staff to provide personalized service and offer special amenities or services to enhance the guest experience.

Partner with Local Businesses

Partnering with local businesses is a great way for hotels to attract more guests and increase revenue. Local businesses can offer exclusive deals or discounts to hotel guests, which can be promoted by the hotel.

For example, The Waldorf Astoria Hotel in New York has partnered with local businesses to create a "Shop and Stay" package. This package includes accommodation at the hotel and discounts at select local stores.

A distressed hotel could partner with local businesses to offer exclusive deals or discounts to guests. For example, they could partner with a local restaurant to offer a free appetizer or dessert to hotel guests. This partnership can benefit both the hotel and the local business, as it can increase revenue for both.

Attend Trade Shows and Events

Attending trade shows and events is a great way for hotels to network with other professionals in the industry and promote their hotel to potential guests.

For example, The Ritz-Carlton Hotel in Washington D.C. attends the annual National Cherry Blossom Festival, which attracts over a million visitors each year. They offer special packages and promotions to festival attendees, which increases their visibility and attracts new guests.

A distressed hotel could attend trade shows and events to promote their hotel to potential guests. They could offer special deals or packages to event attendees or create partnerships with other vendors at the event.

In conclusion, increasing marketing efforts for a distressed hotel requires a multi-faceted approach that includes market research, developing a unique value proposition, digital marketing strategies, offering packages and special deals, using influencer marketing, providing exceptional customer service, partnering with local businesses, and attending trade shows and events. These strategies can be used to improve guest satisfaction, attract new guests, and increase revenue for the hotel. By implementing these strategies, a distressed hotel can overcome financial difficulties and thrive in the competitive hospitality industry.

Chapter 9

Improve Online Reputation

Online reputation is an important factor in the success of a hotel. By improving online reviews and ratings, hotel owners can attract more guests and increase occupancy rates.

Example: The W Chicago Lakeshore hotel was suffering from poor online reviews due to issues with cleanliness and customer service. The owner implemented a new cleaning protocol and invested in staff training to improve customer service. As a result, the hotel's online reputation improved, and occupancy rates increased.

In today's digitally advanced world, the internet has become an essential aspect of our lives. It has significantly influenced how businesses operate and how customers perceive them. Online reputation is a critical aspect of a business's success, especially in the hospitality industry, where customer satisfaction is vital. A distressed hotel is one that is experiencing difficulties in its operations, resulting in poor customer reviews and low occupancy rates. In such a situation, the hotel needs to improve its online reputation to attract more customers and increase its revenue. This chapter discusses how to improve online reputation for a distressed hotel, using examples of each statement.

Monitor online reviews and social media

Monitoring online reviews and social media is a crucial step in improving the online reputation of a distressed hotel. Social media platforms such as Facebook, Twitter, and Instagram provide an excellent opportunity for hotels to interact with customers, address their complaints, and receive feedback. Online review platforms such as TripAdvisor, Yelp, and Google Reviews also allow customers to share their experiences and rate the hotel's services.

One example of a hotel that has effectively monitored online reviews and social media is the Ritz-Carlton hotel. The hotel uses social media to respond to customer complaints and inquiries promptly. In addition, the hotel regularly monitors online reviews and responds to them appropriately. This approach has helped the hotel to maintain a positive online reputation and attract more customers.

Respond to negative reviews

Negative reviews can significantly impact a hotel's online reputation. Responding to negative reviews is crucial in improving the hotel's online reputation. Responding to negative reviews shows that the hotel cares about its customers and is willing to address their complaints. Responding to negative reviews also provides an opportunity for the hotel to explain its side of the story and offer solutions to the customer's complaints.

An example of a hotel that has effectively responded to negative reviews is the Four Seasons Hotel. The hotel responds to negative reviews promptly, addresses the customer's complaints, and offers solutions. The hotel's approach has helped it to maintain a positive online reputation and attract more customers.

Offer exceptional customer service

Offering exceptional customer service is critical in improving the online reputation of a distressed hotel. Exceptional customer service can help to turn dissatisfied customers into loyal customers who are willing to leave positive reviews about the hotel's services. Providing excellent customer service involves going above and beyond to meet customer needs, being attentive to their complaints, and providing solutions.

One example of a hotel that offers exceptional customer service is the St. Regis hotel. The hotel provides personalized service to its guests, anticipates their needs, and goes above and beyond to meet their expectations. This approach has helped the hotel to maintain a positive online reputation and attract more customers.

Use social media to promote positive reviews

Social media provides an excellent opportunity for hotels to promote positive reviews and improve their online reputation. Hotels can share positive reviews on their social media pages and encourage customers to share their experiences on these platforms. Sharing positive reviews on social media platforms can help to increase brand awareness, attract more customers, and improve the hotel's online reputation.

One example of a hotel that has effectively used social media to promote positive reviews is the Marriott hotel. The hotel shares positive reviews on its social media pages and encourages customers to share their experiences on these platforms. This approach has helped the hotel to maintain a positive online reputation and attract more customers.

Implement a reputation management system

Implementing a reputation management system can help to improve the online reputation of a distressed hotel. A reputation management system involves monitoring online reviews and social media, responding to negative reviews, and promoting positive reviews. A reputation management system can also help hotels to identify areas that need improvement and address customer complaints promptly.

One example of a hotel that has effectively implemented a reputation management system is the Hyatt hotel. The hotel uses a reputation management system to monitor online reviews and social media, respond to negative reviews promptly, and promote positive reviews. The hotel also uses customer feedback to identify areas that need improvement and make changes accordingly. This approach has helped the hotel to maintain a positive online reputation and attract more customers.

Offer incentives for positive reviews

Offering incentives for positive reviews can help to improve the online reputation of a distressed hotel. Hotels can offer incentives such as discounts, free upgrades, or loyalty points to customers who leave positive reviews about their services. Offering incentives for positive reviews can encourage customers to share their experiences and leave positive reviews, which can improve the hotel's online reputation.

One example of a hotel that has effectively

offered incentives for positive reviews is the Hilton hotel. The hotel offers loyalty points to customers who leave positive reviews on their website. This approach has helped the hotel to maintain a positive online reputation and attract more customers.

Improve hotel facilities and services

Improving hotel facilities and services is critical in improving the online reputation of a distressed hotel. Hotels should regularly evaluate their facilities and services and make changes to improve customer satisfaction. Improving hotel facilities and services can help to address customer complaints, improve customer experience, and attract more customers.

One example of a hotel that has effectively improved its facilities and services is the Mandarin Oriental hotel. The hotel regularly updates its facilities and services to meet customer needs and improve customer satisfaction. This approach has helped the hotel to maintain a positive online reputation and attract more customers.

Implement a customer loyalty program

Implementing a customer loyalty program can help to improve the online reputation of a distressed hotel. A customer loyalty program can encourage customers to return to the hotel and leave positive reviews about their services. Customer loyalty programs can also help hotels to retain customers and improve customer satisfaction.

One example of a hotel that has effectively implemented a customer loyalty program is the InterContinental hotel. The hotel offers loyalty points to customers who book directly with them and offers exclusive benefits to members of its loyalty program. This approach has helped the hotel to maintain a positive online reputation and attract more customers.

In conclusion, improving the online reputation of a distressed hotel is critical in attracting more customers and increasing revenue. Hotels can improve their online reputation by monitoring online reviews and social media, responding to negative reviews, offering exceptional customer service, using social media to promote positive reviews, implementing a reputation management system, offering incentives for positive reviews, improving hotel facilities and services, and implementing a customer loyalty program. By implementing these strategies, distressed hotels can improve their online reputation and compete effectively in the hospitality industry.

Chapter 10

Develop Partnerships with Local Businesses

Developing partnerships with local businesses can help hotels to attract more guests and increase occupancy rates. This can include partnerships with restaurants, attractions, and other businesses.

Example: The Grand Hyatt in Washington, D.C. developed a partnership with a local restaurant to offer a special dining package for guests. This partnership helped to attract more guests to the hotel and increase occupancy rates.

Hotels are one of the most popular and critical segments of the hospitality industry. However, the hotel industry has been hit hard by the COVID-19 pandemic, which has led to a reduction in travel and a subsequent decrease in hotel occupancy. Many hotels are facing financial difficulties, particularly those in less popular tourist destinations. As a result, distressed hotels need to collaborate with local businesses to increase their market share and remain competitive.

This chapter will discuss how to develop

partnerships with local businesses to help a distressed hotel recover. The first section will define what is meant by a distressed hotel, the second section will examine the benefits of partnering with local businesses, and the third section will provide examples of different types of partnerships that can be developed with local businesses.

Benefits of Partnering with Local Businesses

Partnering with local businesses can provide a range of benefits for distressed hotels. Firstly, it can help to increase the hotel's visibility and reputation within the local community. By working with local businesses, hotels can reach out to a wider audience and build relationships with potential customers. This can lead to increased brand awareness and loyalty, which is important for sustaining long-term success.

Secondly, partnering with local businesses can help to increase revenue streams for distressed hotels. By collaborating with other businesses, hotels can develop new products and services that are tailored to the local market. For example, a hotel could partner with a local tour operator to offer guests discounted tours of the local area. This would not only provide an additional revenue stream for the hotel but also enhance the guest experience.

Finally, partnerships with local businesses can help to reduce costs for distressed hotels. By working together, businesses can share resources and reduce overheads. For example, a hotel could collaborate with a local restaurant to offer guests discounted meals. This would help to reduce the hotel's food and beverage costs while providing guests with a wider range of dining options.

Examples of Partnerships with Local Businesses

Partnership with a Local Tour Operator

One type of partnership that a distressed hotel could develop is with a local tour operator. By collaborating with a tour operator, the hotel could offer guests discounted tours of the local area. This would not only provide an additional revenue stream for the hotel but also enhance the guest experience.

For example, the Malmaison Hotel in Belfast, Northern Ireland, has partnered with Belfast City Sightseeing to offer guests discounted bus tours of the city. Guests can purchase tickets for the tour at the hotel reception desk, and the tour bus picks up and drops off guests at the hotel. This partnership has helped to increase the hotel's visibility within the local community and attract more guests.

Partnership with a Local Restaurant

Another type of partnership that a distressed hotel could develop is with a local restaurant. By collaborating with a restaurant, the hotel could offer guests discounted meals and reduce its food and beverage costs. This would also provide guests with a wider range of dining options, which would enhance the guest experience.

For example, the Royal Garden Hotel in London has partnered with Min Jiang, a Chinese restaurant located next door to the hotel. Guests at the hotel can enjoy a 15% discount on meals at Min Jiang, and the restaurant provides room service for guests staying at the hotel. This partnership has helped to increase revenue streams for both the hotel and the restaurant and provide guests with a more diverse dining experience.

Partnership with a Local Event Venue

A distressed hotel could also develop a partnership with a local event venue to increase its revenue streams. By collaborating with an event venue, the hotel could offer guests discounted tickets to events, as well as provide accommodation for attendees.

For example, the St. Regis Hotel in San Francisco has partnered with the San Francisco Symphony to offer guests discounted tickets to concerts. The hotel also provides accommodation for the symphony's performers and staff during their visits to the city. This partnership has helped to increase the hotel's visibility within the local community and attract more guests, as well as providing a valuable service to the symphony.

Partnership with a Local Spa

Another type of partnership that a distressed

hotel could develop is with a local spa. By collaborating with a spa, the hotel could offer guests discounted spa treatments and enhance the guest experience. This would also help to increase revenue streams for the hotel.

For example, the Conrad Hotel in Miami has partnered with the Tierra Santa Healing House to offer guests discounted spa treatments. The hotel provides complimentary access to the spa's facilities, including its hydrotherapy circuit and thermal suite. This partnership has helped to attract more guests to the hotel and provide them with a more luxurious and relaxing experience.

Partnership with a Local Brewery or Distillery

A distressed hotel could also develop a partnership with a local brewery or distillery to provide guests with a unique and authentic local experience. By collaborating with a brewery or distillery, the hotel could offer guests discounted tours and tastings, as well as provide accommodation for attendees.

For example, the Ace Hotel in Pittsburgh has partnered with the Wigle Whiskey Distillery to offer guests discounted tours and tastings of the distillery. The hotel also provides accommodation for attendees of Wigle's events, such as cocktail-making classes and whiskey tastings. This partnership has helped to increase the hotel's visibility within the local community and attract more guests, as well as providing a valuable service to Wigle.

In conclusion, distressed hotels can benefit greatly from developing partnerships with local businesses. By collaborating with other businesses, hotels can increase their visibility and reputation within the local community, as well as increase their revenue streams and reduce their costs. There are many different types of partnerships that a hotel could develop with local businesses, including partnerships with tour operators, restaurants, event venues, spas, and breweries or distilleries. These partnerships provide a valuable service to both the hotel and the local businesses, as well as enhancing the guest experience. Developing partnerships with local businesses is an important strategy for distressed hotels to remain competitive and recover from financial difficulties.

Chapter 11

Offer Packages and Promotions

Offering packages and promotions can help hotels to attract more guests and increase occupancy rates. This can include discounts, special offers, and package deals.

Example: The Mandarin Oriental in Boston offers a "Stay and Spa" package that includes a spa treatment and overnight accommodations. This package has been successful in attracting more guests to the hotel.

The hotel industry is highly competitive, with numerous players striving to attract guests and generate revenues. Despite the many challenges faced by the industry, including the COVID-19 pandemic, hotels must remain innovative to remain relevant and profitable. Offering packages and promotions is an effective way for hotels to attract new customers, increase revenues, and retain existing customers. In this chapter, we will explore how to offer packages and promotions for a distressed hotel, highlighting the strategies and tactics that can be employed to achieve the desired results.

Part 1: Understanding the Market

The first step in offering packages and promotions for a distressed hotel is to understand the market. The hotel industry is highly dynamic, with changes in customer preferences, competition, and economic conditions influencing demand. Therefore, hotels must conduct market research to determine the needs and preferences of their target customers, identify trends in the industry, and assess the strengths and weaknesses of their competitors.

One way to conduct market research is to use surveys and questionnaires to gather information from existing and potential customers. The survey can cover areas such as customer preferences for room types, amenities, food and beverage, and activities. It can also seek to identify the factors that influence customer decisions when choosing a hotel, such as price, location, and brand reputation.

Another way to gather market information is to use online tools, such as social media and web analytics, to track customer behavior and engagement. For example, hotels can monitor their social media pages to identify the most popular posts, the level of engagement, and the types of comments received. This information can help hotels to tailor their packages and promotions to the needs and preferences of their target customers.

A case in point is the Grand Hyatt Melbourne, which used market research to develop a package that appeals to travelers who are looking for relaxation and rejuvenation. The hotel conducted a survey that revealed that most of its guests were seeking ways to unwind and de-stress. Armed with this information, the hotel created a "Relaxation Package" that includes a one-hour massage, access to the hotel's swimming pool, and a complimentary bottle of wine. This package has proved to be popular with guests, and it has helped the hotel to increase its occupancy rate and revenues.

Part 2: Developing Packages and Promotions

Once a hotel has gathered information about its target market, it can proceed to develop packages and promotions that meet the needs and preferences of its customers. The packages and promotions should be designed to provide value for money, differentiate the hotel from its competitors, and align with the hotel's brand values and positioning.

One way to create packages and promotions is to bundle products and services that are complementary or have a high perceived value. For example, a hotel can create a "Romantic Getaway Package" that includes a bottle of champagne, a box of chocolates, a candlelit dinner, and a couples' massage. This package appeals to couples who are looking for a romantic and intimate experience, and it provides a higher value proposition than if the services were purchased individually.

Another way to develop packages and promotions is to offer discounts or incentives that encourage customers to book directly with the hotel. For example, a hotel can offer a "Direct Booking Promotion" that gives customers a 10% discount on their room rate if they book directly on the hotel's website. This promotion encourages customers to bypass third-party booking sites, which can be expensive for the hotel, and it helps to build a direct relationship with customers.

A third way to create packages and promotions is to align them with the hotel's brand values and positioning. For example, a hotel that positions itself as a luxury and exclusive brand can create a "Luxury Experience Package" that includes a limousine transfer, a personal butler, and access to exclusive amenities, such as a private rooftop terrace. This package will appeal to customers who value exclusivity and luxury, and it reinforces the hotel's brand positioning.

Part 3: Promoting Packages and Promotions

Once a hotel has developed packages and promotions, it must promote them effectively to its target market. Effective promotion is essential to ensure that the packages and promotions reach the right audience and generate the desired results.

One way to promote packages and promotions is to use digital marketing channels, such as social media, email marketing, and online advertising. Social media platforms, such as Facebook and Instagram, provide an excellent opportunity for hotels to showcase their packages and promotions, and to target specific demographics with paid advertising. Email marketing is another effective way to promote packages and promotions, as it allows hotels to communicate directly with customers who have opted in to receive promotional emails. Online advertising, such as Google Ads, can also be used to target customers who are searching for hotels in a particular location or with specific amenities.

Another way to promote packages and promotions is to use traditional marketing channels, such as print media and direct mail. Print media, such as newspapers and magazines, can be used to reach a broader audience, and direct mail can be used to target specific segments of the market, such as loyalty program members or previous customers.

A third way to promote packages and promotions is to partner with other businesses, such as airlines, travel agencies, and tour operators. Partnering with these businesses allows hotels to reach a wider audience and to tap into their existing customer base. For example, a hotel can partner with an airline to offer a "Fly and Stay Package" that includes a discounted airfare and a hotel stay. This package appeals to customers who are looking for convenience and value, and it helps to increase the visibility of the hotel among the airline's customers.

Part 4: Measuring and Evaluating Results

The final step in offering packages and promotions for a distressed hotel is to measure and evaluate the results. Measuring and evaluating results is essential to determine the effectiveness of the packages and promotions, to identify areas for improvement, and to refine the hotel's marketing strategy.

One way to measure and evaluate results is to track key performance indicators (KPIs), such as occupancy rate, revenue per available room (RevPAR), and average daily rate (ADR). These KPIs provide a snapshot of the hotel's performance and can help to identify trends and areas for improvement. For example, if the occupancy rate increases after the introduction of a new package, it suggests that the package is resonating with the target market and generating demand.

Another way to measure and evaluate results is to gather customer feedback through surveys and online reviews. Customer feedback provides valuable insights into the customer experience and can help hotels to identify areas for improvement. For example, if customers consistently complain about the quality of the food in a package that includes meals, it suggests that the hotel needs to improve its food offering.

A third way to measure and evaluate results is to conduct A/B testing, which involves testing two versions of a package or promotion to determine which one performs better. For example, a hotel can test two versions of a "Stay and Play Package" that includes a round of golf. Version A includes a free golf cart rental, while Version B includes a discounted golf cart rental. By tracking the booking and revenue data for each version, the hotel can determine which one generates more revenue and adjust its marketing strategy accordingly.

As previously stated, offering packages and promotions is an effective way for distressed hotels to attract new customers, increase revenues, and retain existing customers. To offer successful packages and promotions, hotels must first understand their target market, develop packages and promotions that provide value for money and align with their brand values, promote them effectively through various marketing channels, and measure and evaluate the results. By following these steps, distressed hotels can position themselves competitively in the market and regain their profitability.

Examples of Packages and Promotions for a Distressed Hotel

To illustrate the concepts discussed in this essay,

we will provide some examples of packages and promotions that a distressed hotel could offer to attract and retain customers.

Example 1: Staycation Package

With the COVID-19 pandemic, many travelers are looking for local getaways instead of international travel. To tap into this market, a distressed hotel could offer a "Staycation Package" that includes a two-night stay, breakfast for two, a complimentary bottle of wine, and a $50 credit for on-site dining or spa services. This package provides value for money and appeals to customers who are looking for a relaxing getaway close to home.

To promote this package, the hotel could use digital marketing channels, such as social media and email marketing, to target customers who live within a certain radius of the hotel. The hotel could also partner with local businesses, such as restaurants and attractions, to create a "Staycation Guide" that includes recommendations for local activities and dining options.

To measure and evaluate the results of this package, the hotel could track its occupancy rate, RevPAR, and ADR during the promotion period. The hotel could also gather customer feedback through surveys and online reviews to identify areas for improvement.

Example 2: Wellness Retreat Package

Wellness tourism is a growing trend, and many travelers are looking for hotels that offer wellness amenities and activities. To tap into this market, a distressed hotel could offer a "Wellness Retreat Package" that includes a two-night stay, daily yoga or fitness classes, a spa treatment, and a healthy meal plan.

To promote this package, the hotel could use digital marketing channels, such as social media and online advertising, to target customers who are interested in wellness and fitness. The hotel could also partner with local wellness businesses, such as yoga studios and health food stores, to offer discounts and promotions.

To measure and evaluate the results of this package, the hotel could track its occupancy rate, RevPAR, and ADR during the promotion period. The hotel could also conduct A/B testing to determine which version of the package generates more revenue, such as testing two different spa treatments or meal plans.

Example 3: Loyalty Program Promotion

Loyalty programs are a powerful tool for retaining existing customers and generating repeat business. To incentivize customers to join its loyalty program, a distressed hotel could offer a promotion that rewards customers with points or discounts for signing up.

To promote this promotion, the hotel could use traditional marketing channels, such as print media and direct mail, to target previous customers and loyalty program members. The hotel could also use digital marketing channels, such as email marketing and social media, to reach a broader audience and offer exclusive promotions for loyalty program members.

To measure and evaluate the results of this promotion, the hotel could track the number of new loyalty program sign-ups and the revenue generated by these customers. The hotel could also gather customer feedback through surveys and online reviews to identify areas for improvement in the loyalty program.

In conclusion, offering packages and promotions is a powerful tool for distressed hotels to attract new customers, increase revenues, and retain existing customers. By understanding their target market, developing packages and promotions that provide value for money and align with their brand values, promoting them effectively through various marketing channels, and measuring and evaluating the results, distressed hotels can position themselves competitively in the market and regain their profitability. The examples provided in this essay demonstrate the versatility and effectiveness of packages and promotions in addressing different customer needs and preferences.

Chapter 12

Develop a Loyalty Program

Loyalty programs can help to increase repeat business and attract new guests. By offering rewards and incentives to loyal customers, hotels can encourage them to book their next stay at the property.

Example: The Hilton Honors loyalty program offers members exclusive benefits, including free room upgrades and late checkout. This program has been successful in increasing customer loyalty and attracting new guests to Hilton properties.

The hospitality industry has witnessed a significant shift in the last decade due to increased competition, advancements in technology, and the entry of new players. Hotels, in particular, have struggled to maintain their competitive edge, with many experiencing a decline in occupancy rates and revenues. In response, hoteliers have resorted to implementing loyalty programs to attract and retain customers. A loyalty program is a marketing strategy designed to encourage customers to become repeat clients by offering incentives and rewards for their loyalty. This chapter aims to explore how to develop a loyalty program for a distressed hotel and provide examples of each statement.

Understand the customer base

To develop a successful loyalty program, it is essential to understand the target customer base. This involves analyzing the demographics, preferences, and behavior of guests who frequent the hotel. For instance, if the hotel attracts business travelers, the loyalty program should be designed to cater to their needs, such as offering a complimentary meeting room or providing express check-in and check-out services. If the hotel attracts families, the loyalty program could offer perks such as free breakfast, complimentary babysitting services, or discounted rates for children's activities.

Example: Best Western Rewards

Best Western Rewards is a loyalty program that is tailored to meet the needs of different types of customers. The program offers four different levels of membership, including Blue, Gold, Platinum, and

Diamond. Members can earn points for their stays, which can be redeemed for free nights, airline miles, gift cards, and other rewards. The program also offers perks such as early check-in and late check-out, room upgrades, and bonus points for elite members. By understanding the needs of its customer base, Best Western Rewards has developed a loyalty program that appeals to a wide range of guests.

Define the program's objectives

Before developing a loyalty program, it is essential to define its objectives. The program's objectives should align with the hotel's overall marketing and business goals. For instance, if the hotel is looking to increase occupancy rates, the loyalty program could be designed to incentivize guests to book their next stay directly with the hotel. If the hotel is looking to increase revenue, the loyalty program could offer incentives for guests to spend more money at the hotel's restaurant or spa.

Example: Marriott Bonvoy

Marriott Bonvoy is a loyalty program that is designed to drive customer loyalty and increase revenue. The program offers members the ability to earn points for their stays, which can be redeemed for free nights, room upgrades, and other rewards. The program also offers exclusive member rates, early check-in, and late check-out. By incentivizing members to book directly with Marriott, the program helps the hotel chain increase its revenue and reduce commission costs.

Determine the program's structure

The structure of the loyalty program refers to the rules, requirements, and benefits of the program. The program's structure should be easy to understand, transparent, and fair. It should also be flexible enough to accommodate different types of customers and their needs. For instance, the program could offer multiple ways to earn and redeem points, such as through stays, dining, or spa services. The program should also have a tiered structure, with different levels of membership and benefits.

Example: Hilton Honors

Hilton Honors is a loyalty program that has a clear and straightforward structure. Members can earn points for their stays, which can be redeemed for free nights, room upgrades, and other rewards. The program also has a tiered structure, with four different levels of membership, including Member, Silver, Gold, and Diamond. Each level offers different benefits, such as late check-out, free breakfast, and access to executive lounges. By having a clear and flexible structure, Hilton Honors has developed a loyalty program that is easy to understand and appeals to a wide range of customers.

Offer valuable rewards and incentives

To incentivize customers to participate in the

loyalty program, it is essential to offer valuable rewards and incentives. The rewards should be relevant to the customer base and reflect their preferences and needs. The incentives could include free nights, room upgrades, discounts on future stays, free amenities, and other perks. The rewards should also be attainable and achievable, so customers feel motivated to participate in the program.

Example: Accor Live Limitless

Accor Live Limitless is a loyalty program that offers valuable rewards and incentives to its members. Members can earn points for their stays, which can be redeemed for free nights, room upgrades, and other rewards. The program also offers exclusive member rates, early check-in, and late check-out. In addition, members can earn points through dining, spa services, and other activities. The program also has a partnership with airline companies, allowing members to earn airline miles for their stays. By offering a range of valuable rewards and incentives, Accor Live Limitless has developed a loyalty program that attracts and retains customers.

Communicate effectively with members

To maintain the loyalty program's effectiveness, it is essential to communicate effectively with members. The hotel should keep members informed about their point balance, rewards, and other program updates. The hotel should also solicit feedback from members and use it to improve the program's structure and rewards.

Effective communication could include newsletters, email updates, and personalized messages.

Example: IHG Rewards Club

IHG Rewards Club is a loyalty program that communicates effectively with its members. Members receive regular email updates about their point balance, new offers, and other program updates. The program also sends personalized messages to members, such as birthday greetings and special offers. In addition, the program solicits feedback from members through surveys and other means. By communicating effectively with members, IHG Rewards Club has developed a loyal customer base that is engaged with the program.

In conclusion, developing a loyalty program for a distressed hotel is an effective marketing strategy that can attract and retain customers. To develop a successful loyalty program, the hotel should understand its customer base, define the program's objectives, determine the program's structure, offer valuable rewards and incentives, and communicate effectively with members. Examples of successful loyalty programs include Best Western Rewards, Marriott Bonvoy, Hilton Honors, Accor Live Limitless, and IHG Rewards Club. By following these guidelines and learning from these examples, a distressed hotel can develop a loyalty program that is tailored to its customer base and helps the hotel achieve its marketing and business goals.

Chapter 13

Reduction of Costs and Expenses

Reducing costs is an important part of turning around a distressed hotel. By reducing expenses, hotel owners can increase profits and improve the property's financial performance.

Example: The Sheraton New York Times Square hotel was suffering from declining revenues and high expenses. The owner implemented cost-cutting measures, including reducing staff and renegotiating contracts with suppliers. As a result, the hotel's financial performance improved.

Hotels, like any other business, can go through tough financial times. This is especially true during times of economic downturns or periods of low occupancy rates. During these times, hotel management is faced with the challenge of reducing costs and spending while still maintaining the quality of service that guests expect. In this chapter, we will discuss some strategies that hotel management can use to reduce costs and spending for a distressed hotel. We will use examples of each strategy to illustrate how they can be applied in practice.

Implement Energy Conservation Measures

One of the most effective ways to reduce costs for a distressed hotel is by implementing energy conservation measures. These measures can help to reduce energy consumption, which in turn reduces energy bills. Some of the energy conservation measures that hotel management can implement include:

a. Replacing old lighting fixtures with LED lights: LED lights are more energy-efficient than traditional lighting fixtures. By replacing old lighting fixtures with LED lights, hotels can reduce their energy consumption and save money on their energy bills.

b. Installing motion sensors: Installing motion sensors in common areas such as hallways and conference rooms can help to ensure that lights are only on when they are needed. This can help to reduce energy consumption and save money on energy bills.

c. Using energy-efficient appliances: Replacing old appliances with energy-efficient ones can help to reduce energy consumption and save money on energy bills. For example, hotels can replace old refrigerators with energy-efficient ones that use less energy.

Example: The Four Seasons Hotel, Sydney

The Four Seasons Hotel in Sydney implemented a range of energy conservation measures to reduce its energy consumption and save money on energy bills. These measures included replacing old lighting fixtures with LED lights, installing motion sensors in common areas, and using energy-efficient appliances. As a result of these measures, the hotel was able to reduce its energy consumption by 18% and save approximately $170,000 per year in energy bills.

Optimize Staffing Levels

Another strategy that hotel management can use to reduce costs and spending for a distressed hotel is by optimizing staffing levels. This involves ensuring that the hotel has the right number of staff to meet the needs of guests without overstaffing. Overstaffing can lead to unnecessary labor costs, which can eat into the hotel's profits.

To optimize staffing levels, hotel management can use a range of tools and techniques. These include:

a. Labor forecasting: Labor forecasting involves predicting how many staff will be needed to meet the needs of guests. This can be done using historical data on occupancy rates and staffing levels.

b. Scheduling software: Scheduling software can help hotel management to create staff schedules that optimize staffing levels. This software can take into account factors such as occupancy rates and staff availability.

c. Cross-training staff: Cross-training staff can help to ensure that the hotel has the right mix of skills to meet the needs of guests. This can help to reduce the need for additional staff and save money on labor costs.

Example: The W New York Hotel

The W New York Hotel implemented a range of

staffing optimization measures to reduce its labor costs. These measures included labor forecasting, scheduling software, and cross-training staff. As a result of these measures, the hotel was able to reduce its labor costs by 15% and increase its profits by approximately $1.5 million per year.

Renegotiate Contracts

Another strategy that hotel management can use to reduce costs and spending for a distressed hotel is by renegotiating contracts with suppliers and vendors. This can help to reduce the cost of goods and services that the hotel purchases, which in turn can reduce the hotel's operating costs.

To renegotiate contracts, hotel management can use a range of tactics. These include:

a. Comparison shopping: Comparison shopping involves comparing the prices of goods and services from different suppliers and choosing the supplier with the most competitive prices. This can help to reduce the cost of goods and services that the hotel purchases.

b. Negotiation: Negotiation involves discussing the terms of a contract with a supplier or vendor and seeking to negotiate more favorable terms. This can include negotiating lower prices, longer payment terms, or better service levels.

c. Consolidation: Consolidation involves

consolidating purchases with one supplier or vendor. This can help to reduce administrative costs and increase purchasing power, which can lead to lower prices.

Example: The Ritz-Carlton Hotel, San Francisco

The Ritz-Carlton Hotel in San Francisco implemented a range of contract renegotiation measures to reduce its operating costs. These measures included comparison shopping, negotiation, and consolidation. As a result of these measures, the hotel was able to reduce its operating costs by 10% and save approximately $500,000 per year.

Reduce Food and Beverage Costs

Food and beverage costs can be a significant expense for hotels. To reduce these costs, hotel management can use a range of strategies. These include:

a. Menu optimization: Menu optimization involves reviewing the menu and identifying items that are not selling well. These items can be removed from the menu to reduce waste and lower food costs.

b. Negotiating with suppliers: Negotiating with suppliers can help to reduce the cost of food and beverages that the hotel purchases. This can include negotiating lower prices or seeking out alternative suppliers.

c. Implementing portion control: Implementing

portion control can help to reduce food waste and lower food costs. This involves ensuring that portions are not too large and that food is not being wasted.

Example: The Ritz-Carlton Hotel, Hong Kong

The Ritz-Carlton Hotel in Hong Kong implemented a range of food and beverage cost reduction measures to reduce its operating costs. These measures included menu optimization, negotiating with suppliers, and implementing portion control. As a result of these measures, the hotel was able to reduce its food and beverage costs by 12% and save approximately $300,000 per year.

Implement Revenue Management Strategies

Implementing revenue management strategies can help hotel management to optimize room rates and maximize revenue. This can be particularly important for distressed hotels that may be experiencing low occupancy rates.

To implement revenue management strategies, hotel management can use a range of tactics. These include:

a. Dynamic pricing: Dynamic pricing involves adjusting room rates based on demand. This can help to ensure that room rates are competitive and that the hotel is maximizing revenue.

b.   Overbooking: Overbooking involves accepting more reservations than the hotel has available rooms. This can help to ensure that the hotel is fully occupied and that revenue is maximized.

c.   Yield management: Yield management involves adjusting room rates based on the length of stay and other factors. This can help to ensure that the hotel is maximizing revenue from each guest.

Example: The Peninsula Hotel, Chicago

The Peninsula Hotel in Chicago implemented a range of revenue management strategies to optimize its room rates and maximize revenue. These strategies included dynamic pricing, overbooking, and yield management. As a result of these measures, the hotel was able to increase its revenue per available room (RevPAR) by 8% and increase its profits by approximately $2.5 million per year.

In conclusion, reducing costs and spending for a distressed hotel can be a challenging task. However, by implementing a range of strategies, hotel management can reduce costs and improve profitability. These strategies include implementing energy conservation measures, optimizing staffing levels, renegotiating contracts, reducing food and beverage costs, and implementing revenue management strategies. By using these strategies, hotels can reduce costs and improve profitability, even during times of economic downturns or low occupancy rates.

Chapter 14

Increase Operational Efficiency

Improving efficiency can help to reduce costs and improve the property's financial performance. This can include streamlining operations, reducing waste, and optimizing staffing levels.

Example: The Hilton San Francisco Union Square hotel implemented a new technology system that helped to streamline operations and reduce waste. This new system has helped to improve the hotel's efficiency and reduce costs.

Operational efficiency is a vital factor for any hotel's success. However, maintaining operational efficiency in a distressed hotel is quite challenging. In such a situation, the hotel needs to optimize its resources and adopt new strategies to ensure efficiency. In this chapter, we will discuss how to increase operational efficiency for a distressed hotel. We will explore various strategies and provide examples of each statement.

Streamline Operations:

The first step towards improving operational efficiency in a distressed hotel is to streamline operations. This includes identifying unnecessary tasks and eliminating them, consolidating redundant roles, and optimizing workflows. For example, the hotel could automate the check-in process to reduce the time spent on this task. This would free up the front desk staff to focus on other essential tasks, such as attending to guests' needs.

Adopt Technology:

Another way to increase operational efficiency is to adopt technology. The hotel could invest in a property management system (PMS) to streamline operations. A PMS can automate tasks such as room allocation, inventory management, and billing. This would reduce errors and save time, allowing staff to focus on more critical tasks. For example, the Marriott chain of hotels uses a mobile app that allows guests to check-in, check-out, and access their room key through their smartphones. This reduces the workload on the front desk staff and enhances the guest experience.

Cross-train Staff:

Cross-training staff is another way to increase operational efficiency. In a distressed hotel, the staff may have to perform tasks outside their usual roles. Cross-training ensures that staff can perform multiple tasks, reducing the need for additional staff. For example, a front desk clerk who is trained to operate the hotel's laundry equipment can assist in the laundry room during busy periods.

Reduce Staff Turnover:

Reducing staff turnover is critical to maintaining operational efficiency. In a distressed hotel, staff turnover can be high, leading to a loss of institutional knowledge and the need to retrain new staff. Offering competitive compensation packages and investing in staff training and development can help reduce turnover. For example, the Four Seasons hotel chain has a comprehensive training program that prepares staff to deliver exceptional service. This has helped reduce staff turnover and improve operational efficiency.

Implement Energy Efficiency Measures:

Implementing energy efficiency measures is another way to increase operational efficiency. This includes measures such as installing energy-efficient lighting and HVAC systems, using low-flow showerheads and faucets, and encouraging guests to reuse towels and linens. These measures can reduce energy consumption and water usage, lowering utility bills and reducing the hotel's environmental footprint. For example, the Hilton hotel chain has implemented a program called LightStay, which tracks energy and water usage at its properties worldwide. This program has helped the chain reduce energy consumption by 10% and water usage by 15%.

Analyze Data:

Analyzing data is essential to increasing operational efficiency. Data analysis can identify inefficiencies and areas for improvement. For example, analyzing guest feedback can help the hotel identify areas where the guest experience can be improved. Similarly, analyzing staff performance data can help identify areas where additional training is needed. The data can also be used to optimize pricing, inventory management, and other aspects of hotel operations. For example, the InterContinental Hotels Group uses data analysis to optimize pricing and yield management, leading to increased revenue and improved operational efficiency.

Focus on Employee Satisfaction:

Focusing on employee satisfaction is critical to maintaining operational efficiency. Satisfied employees are more productive and provide better customer service.

To improve employee satisfaction, the hotel could offer benefits such as flexible scheduling, wellness programs, and opportunities for career advancement. For example, the Ritz-Carlton hotel chain offers a comprehensive wellness program that includes fitness classes, healthy food options, and mental health resources. This has helped improve employee satisfaction and operational efficiency.

Optimize Inventory Management:

Optimizing inventory management is another way to increase operational efficiency. This includes reducing inventory levels, improving inventory accuracy, and optimizing the ordering process. For example, the hotel could implement a just-in-time inventory system that ensures supplies are delivered when needed, reducing the need for excess inventory. This would free up storage space and reduce the cost of carrying inventory. Similarly, the hotel could use barcode scanning technology to improve inventory accuracy and reduce the risk of stockouts.

Enhance Guest Experience:

Enhancing the guest experience is critical to maintaining operational efficiency. Satisfied guests are more likely to return and recommend the hotel to others. To enhance the guest experience, the hotel could invest in training staff to provide exceptional service, improve room cleanliness and comfort, and offer personalized amenities. For example, the Hyatt hotel chain offers a mobile app that allows guests to customize their stay by selecting room preferences, ordering room service, and requesting housekeeping services.

Improve Marketing Strategy:

Improving the hotel's marketing strategy can also increase operational efficiency. A well-crafted marketing strategy can attract new customers and retain existing ones. The hotel could use social media, email marketing, and targeted advertising to reach potential guests. For example, the Four Seasons hotel chain uses social media to engage with customers and promote its properties. This has helped the chain attract new customers and maintain customer loyalty.

Monitor and Measure Performance:

Monitoring and measuring performance is essential to maintaining operational efficiency. The hotel could use key performance indicators (KPIs) to track performance and identify areas for improvement. KPIs could include occupancy rates, average daily rate (ADR), revenue per available room (RevPAR), and customer satisfaction scores. For example, the Marriott hotel chain uses a dashboard that displays KPIs in real-time, allowing staff to monitor performance and make adjustments as needed.

Emphasize Continuous Improvement:

Emphasizing continuous improvement is critical

to maintaining operational efficiency. The hotel should regularly review its processes and identify opportunities for improvement. This could involve soliciting feedback from staff and customers, benchmarking against competitors, and staying up-to-date with industry trends. For example, the Accor hotel chain has implemented a program called Planet 21 that focuses on sustainability and social responsibility. This program has helped the chain improve operational efficiency and enhance its reputation.

In conclusion, increasing operational efficiency in a distressed hotel requires a comprehensive approach that includes streamlining operations, adopting technology, cross-training staff, reducing staff turnover, implementing energy efficiency measures, analyzing data, focusing on employee satisfaction, optimizing inventory management, enhancing the guest experience, improving the marketing strategy, monitoring and measuring performance, and emphasizing continuous improvement. By implementing these strategies, the hotel can reduce costs, improve customer satisfaction, and enhance its reputation, ultimately leading to long-term success.

Chapter 15

Improve Energy Efficiency

Improving energy efficiency can help hotels to reduce costs and improve their environmental impact. This can include implementing energy-efficient lighting and HVAC systems, as well as reducing water consumption.

Example: The Westin St. Francis in San Francisco implemented an energy-efficient lighting system that reduced energy consumption by 60%. This new system has helped to reduce the hotel's operating costs and improve its environmental impact.

Energy efficiency is a critical aspect of sustainable living, and it has become increasingly important in the hospitality industry. Hotels consume a significant amount of energy, with heating, ventilation, and air conditioning (HVAC) systems and lighting being among the most significant energy users. However, many hotels struggle with their energy consumption, leading to high energy bills and reduced profitability. In this chapter, we will discuss how to improve energy efficiency for a distressed hotel, using examples to illustrate each statement.

Assess the hotel's current energy usage

Before implementing any energy efficiency measures, it is essential to conduct an assessment of the hotel's current energy usage. This will help identify areas where energy is being wasted and areas where improvements can be made. A thorough energy audit should include an analysis of the hotel's energy bills, an inspection of the building envelope, and a review of the HVAC, lighting, and water heating systems.

For example, the Hilton Frankfurt City Centre hotel conducted an energy audit and found that it could save up to 35% on energy costs by implementing energy-saving measures. The hotel replaced all of its light bulbs with LED bulbs, installed motion sensors to turn off lights when not in use, and upgraded its HVAC system to a more energy-efficient one.

Upgrade lighting systems

Lighting is one of the most significant energy consumers in a hotel. Upgrading to more energy-efficient lighting systems can result in significant cost savings. LED bulbs are the most energy-efficient lighting option available and have become the industry standard for hotels.

For example, the Marriott International hotel chain has implemented an LED lighting upgrade program across its properties worldwide. The program involves replacing all incandescent bulbs with LED bulbs, resulting in an average energy savings of 50% per room. The Marriott International hotel in Dubai Marina has saved up to 75% on lighting energy costs by upgrading to LED bulbs.

Install occupancy sensors

Occupancy sensors are an effective way to reduce energy consumption in hotel rooms. These sensors detect when a room is occupied and turn off lights and HVAC systems when the room is vacant. This can result in significant energy savings, particularly in guest rooms.

For example, the Sheraton Seattle Hotel installed occupancy sensors in all of its guest rooms and meeting rooms. The sensors are estimated to save the hotel up to $200,000 per year in energy costs.

Upgrade HVAC systems

HVAC systems are a significant energy consumer in hotels, accounting for up to 60% of total energy usage. Upgrading to more energy-efficient HVAC systems can result in significant cost savings.

For example, the Four Seasons Hotel in Vancouver replaced its HVAC system with a more energy-efficient one, resulting in a 37% reduction in energy consumption. The hotel also installed variable frequency drives on its pumps and fans, resulting in an additional 10% reduction in energy consumption.

Implement water-saving measures

Water heating is another significant energy consumer in hotels. Implementing water-saving measures such as low-flow showerheads, faucets, and toilets can result in significant cost savings. These measures not only reduce energy consumption but also conserve water, which is a valuable resource.

For example, the Hyatt Regency Boston installed low-flow showerheads and faucets in all of its guest rooms and public areas. The hotel estimates that these measures will result in an annual water savings of 2.2 million gallons and an annual energy savings of $19,000.

Implement renewable energy systems

Renewable energy systems such as solar and wind power can provide a significant source of clean energy for hotels. Installing solar panels or wind turbines can reduce a hotel's dependence on grid electricity and result in significant cost savings.

For example, the St. Regis Princeville Resort in Hawaii installed a 272-kilowatt solar photovoltaic system, which provides 80% of the hotel's energy needs. The system is estimated to save the hotel over $250,000 per year in energy costs.

Improve building insulation

Building insulation is an essential aspect of

reducing energy consumption in hotels. Proper insulation can help reduce heating and cooling costs, resulting in significant energy savings. Improving insulation can be as simple as sealing air leaks or as extensive as upgrading wall and roof insulation.

For example, the Hilton Anaheim hotel in California implemented a building envelope improvement program that included sealing air leaks, upgrading wall insulation, and installing low-emissivity windows. The program resulted in a 10% reduction in energy consumption and a savings of over $600,000 per year in energy costs.

Educate staff and guests on energy-saving practices

Educating staff and guests on energy-saving practices can help create a culture of energy efficiency in hotels. This can include simple measures such as turning off lights and electronics when not in use, using natural lighting whenever possible, and adjusting HVAC systems to conserve energy.

For example, the Fairmont Banff Springs hotel in Canada has implemented an energy conservation program that includes educating staff and guests on energy-saving practices. The program resulted in a 9% reduction in energy consumption and a savings of over $200,000 per year in energy costs.

In conclusion, improving energy efficiency is essential for distressed hotels to reduce energy costs, increase profitability, and become more sustainable. Implementing energy-saving measures such as upgrading lighting systems, installing occupancy sensors, upgrading HVAC systems, implementing water-saving measures, installing renewable energy systems, improving building insulation, and educating staff and guests can result in significant cost savings and reduce a hotel's carbon footprint. By implementing these measures, distressed hotels can become more competitive, attract environmentally conscious guests, and contribute to a more sustainable future.

Chapter 16

Renovate and Update

Renovating and updating the property can help to attract more guests and improve the hotel's financial performance. This can include updating guest rooms, common areas, and amenities.

Example: The Ritz-Carlton in New York City underwent a $100 million renovation that included updating guest rooms and public spaces. This renovation helped to improve the hotel's image and attract more guests.

The hospitality industry is constantly evolving, and hotel properties need to stay up-to-date with the latest trends to remain competitive. However, it is not uncommon for hotels to become run-down and distressed over time. Renovating and updating a distressed hotel can be a daunting task, but it is necessary to remain relevant in the market. In this chapter, we will discuss how to renovate and update a distressed hotel and provide examples of each statement.

Assess the Property

The first step in renovating a distressed hotel is to assess the property thoroughly. This includes evaluating the condition of the building, the amenities, the decor, and the guest rooms. A comprehensive assessment of the property will provide insight into the areas that need the most attention.

For example, the Grand Hotel in Michigan underwent a renovation that included a thorough assessment of the property. The hotel had been in operation for over 100 years, and many areas needed attention. The renovation team assessed every inch of the property and determined that the guest rooms needed the most attention. The guest rooms were renovated to include modern amenities and decor that would appeal to the modern traveler.

Upgrade the Guest Rooms

One of the most important areas to renovate in a

distressed hotel is the guest rooms. The guest rooms are where guests spend most of their time, and they need to be comfortable and inviting. Upgrading the guest rooms can be done in several ways, such as updating the decor, adding new amenities, or renovating the bathrooms.

For example, the Four Seasons Hotel in New York City underwent a renovation that included upgrading the guest rooms. The hotel installed new flat-screen televisions, updated the bedding and linens, and renovated the bathrooms to include new fixtures and marble accents. These upgrades provided guests with a more luxurious and comfortable experience.

Redesign Public Spaces

Public spaces, such as lobbies and restaurants, are another area that needs attention when renovating a distressed hotel. These areas need to be inviting and comfortable to create a welcoming atmosphere for guests. Redesigning public spaces can include updating the decor, adding new seating, or installing new lighting.

For example, the Ritz Carlton in San Francisco underwent a renovation that included redesigning the lobby and restaurant. The hotel updated the decor to include modern furnishings and artwork, added new seating areas, and installed new lighting fixtures. These upgrades created a more inviting and comfortable atmosphere for guests.

Add New Amenities

Adding new amenities to a distressed hotel can be a great way to attract new guests and retain existing ones. New amenities can include a fitness center, a spa, a rooftop bar, or a pool. Adding new amenities can also help a hotel stand out from the competition.

For example, the Hotel Emma in San Antonio underwent a renovation that included adding new amenities. The hotel added a rooftop bar, a fitness center, and a pool to provide guests with additional options for entertainment and relaxation. These new amenities helped the hotel attract new guests and retain existing ones.

Incorporate Technology

Incorporating technology into a distressed hotel can also be an effective way to attract new guests and create a more comfortable experience for existing ones. Technology can include things like keyless entry, smart thermostats, and voice-controlled devices. Incorporating technology can also help a hotel stand out from the competition.

For example, the CitizenM Hotel in New York City incorporates technology into every aspect of the guest experience. The hotel uses keyless entry, provides guests with tablets to control the room temperature and lighting, and has voice-controlled devices in each room. These technological advancements create a more efficient and comfortable experience for guests.

Consider Sustainability

Sustainability is becoming increasingly important to travelers, and incorporating sustainable practices into a hotel renovation can help attract new guests and create a positive image for the property. Sustainable practices can include things like using renewable energy sources, reducing water waste, and using environmentally friendly materials.

For example, the 1 Hotel Brooklyn Bridge in New York City underwent a renovation that incorporated sustainable practices. The hotel uses renewable energy sources, such as solar panels and wind turbines, to power the property. The hotel also uses reclaimed materials, such as wood from old buildings, to create a unique and sustainable decor. These sustainable practices help the hotel attract environmentally conscious travelers and create a positive image for the property.

Consider Accessibility

Accessibility is an important factor to consider when renovating a hotel. Accessibility can include things like wheelchair ramps, accessible bathrooms, and Braille signage. Making a hotel more accessible can help attract a wider range of guests and create a more inclusive atmosphere.

For example, the Park Hyatt in Tokyo underwent a renovation that included making the property more accessible. The hotel installed wheelchair ramps, accessible bathrooms, and Braille signage to create a more inclusive atmosphere for guests. These accessibility upgrades help the hotel attract a wider range of guests and create a more welcoming environment.

Invest in Marketing

Investing in marketing is essential when renovating a distressed hotel. Marketing can include things like social media campaigns, email marketing, and targeted advertising. Effective marketing can help a hotel attract new guests and create a positive image for the property.

For example, the Fontainebleau Miami Beach underwent a renovation that included investing in marketing. The hotel launched a social media campaign that showcased the new renovations and amenities. The campaign included influencer partnerships and targeted advertising, which helped the hotel attract new guests and create a positive image for the property.

In conclusion, Renovating and updating a distressed hotel can be a challenging task, but it is essential to remain competitive in the market. Assessing the property, upgrading the guest rooms, redesigning public spaces, adding new amenities, incorporating technology, considering sustainability, and making the property more accessible are all effective ways to renovate a distressed hotel. Investing in marketing is also essential to attract new guests and create a positive image for the property. By following these steps and using examples of successful hotel renovations, a distressed hotel can be transformed into a thriving property that attracts new guests and retains existing ones.

Chapter 17

Focus on Group Business

Group business can be a lucrative source of revenue for hotels. By focusing on attracting group bookings, hotel owners can increase occupancy rates and improve financial performance.

Example: The Hyatt Regency Chicago implemented a new sales strategy that focused on attracting group bookings. As a result, the hotel was able to increase its group business by 25% and improve its financial performance.

The hospitality industry has experienced significant disruptions in recent times, ranging from natural disasters, economic downturns, pandemics, and global recessions. These crises can lead to a decrease in hotel occupancy rates, which negatively impact revenue generation. Hotels that are struggling to generate revenue and stay afloat need to adopt various strategies to survive. One strategy that has proven to be effective in such scenarios is to focus on group business. Group business involves catering to the needs of businesses, organizations, or events that require accommodations, meeting spaces, or event venues. In this chapter, we will discuss how a distressed hotel can focus on group business to improve revenue generation, and we will use examples to illustrate each statement.

Understanding the needs of group business clients

The first step to focusing on group business is to understand the needs of the clients. Group business clients are different from individual travelers, and hotels must tailor their services to meet their unique needs. Group business clients are more interested in the quality of meeting spaces, the availability of audio-visual equipment, and the quality of food and beverages. A distressed hotel must prioritize these services to attract group business clients.

For instance, in 2017, the Houstonian Hotel, Club & Spa in Texas faced the challenge of reduced occupancy rates following Hurricane Harvey. The hotel management adopted a strategy of focusing on group business to improve revenue. The hotel management prioritized the needs of group business clients, and this resulted in increased bookings. The hotel upgraded its meeting spaces, added new audio-visual equipment, and improved its food and beverage services. As a result, the Houstonian Hotel, Club & Spa recorded an increase in group business bookings by 30% in 2018.

Networking and building relationships

Networking and building relationships with event planners, travel agents, and meeting planners are crucial for a distressed hotel to attract group business clients. These professionals have a wide network of clients, and if they have a good experience at a particular hotel, they are likely to recommend it to their clients. A distressed hotel must make a concerted effort to network and build relationships with these professionals to improve its chances of attracting group business clients.

For example, the Las Vegas Hilton faced significant financial difficulties in 2009 due to the global recession. The hotel management adopted a strategy of networking and building relationships with meeting planners and event organizers. The hotel management organized familiarization trips for meeting planners and event organizers, where they could experience the hotel's services first-hand. Additionally, the hotel management attended trade shows and conferences where they could meet with these professionals and showcase the hotel's services. As a result, the Las Vegas Hilton attracted more group business clients, and in 2010, the hotel recorded an increase in group business bookings by 15%.

Creating attractive group packages

Creating attractive group packages is another strategy that a distressed hotel can use to attract group business clients. Group packages can include discounts on room rates, food and beverage services, and meeting spaces. A distressed hotel must ensure that the group packages it creates are attractive and offer value for money.

For instance, the Hilton Los Cabos Beach & Golf Resort in Mexico faced a significant decline in occupancy rates following Hurricane Odile in 2014. The hotel management adopted a strategy of creating attractive group packages to attract group business clients. The hotel created packages that included discounted room rates, free meeting spaces, and complimentary breakfast. The hotel also offered a complimentary sunset cocktail hour and discounted spa services. The hotel's efforts paid off, and it recorded an increase in group business bookings by 25% in 2015.

Leveraging technology

Leveraging technology is crucial for a distressed hotel to attract group business clients. Technology can help a hotel streamline its operations and improve its services, making it more attractive to group business clients. For example, a hotel can leverage technology to automate its booking process, offer virtual tours of meeting spaces, and provide audio-visual support during events. A distressed hotel must ensure that its technology is up-to-date and offers the necessary functionalities to cater to the needs of group business clients.

For example, in 2020, the COVID-19 pandemic had a significant impact on the hospitality industry, and hotels had to adopt technology to attract group business clients. The Marriott International hotel chain launched a new virtual events platform called "Connect with Confidence" that enabled virtual meetings and events. The platform offered various features, including virtual tours of meeting spaces, live streaming, and on-demand content. The Marriott International hotel chain's efforts paid off, and it recorded an increase in group business bookings by 20% in 2021.

Emphasizing safety and hygiene protocols

In the current pandemic era, safety and hygiene protocols have become a top priority for group business clients. A distressed hotel must ensure that it has robust safety and hygiene protocols in place to attract group business clients. These protocols can include regular cleaning and sanitization of meeting spaces, providing hand sanitizers, and enforcing social distancing measures.

For instance, in 2020, the JW Marriott Camelback Inn Resort & Spa in Arizona faced a significant decline in occupancy rates following the COVID-19 pandemic. The hotel management adopted a strategy of emphasizing safety and hygiene protocols to attract group business clients. The hotel implemented various safety measures, including frequent cleaning of meeting spaces, providing hand sanitizers, and enforcing social distancing measures. The hotel's efforts paid off, and it recorded an increase in group business bookings by 15% in 2021.

In conclusion, a distressed hotel can focus on group business to improve revenue generation. To achieve this, a distressed hotel must understand the needs of group business clients, network and build relationships with event planners and meeting planners, create attractive group packages, leverage technology, and emphasize safety and hygiene protocols. These strategies have proven to be effective in various scenarios, and hotels that adopt them are likely to attract more group business clients and improve revenue generation.

Chapter 18

Implement Revenue Management Strategies

Revenue management strategies can help hotels to optimize their pricing and increase profitability. This can include dynamic pricing, inventory management, and demand forecasting.

Example: The Hilton Garden Inn in Chicago

implemented a dynamic pricing strategy that adjusted room rates based on demand. This strategy helped to increase the hotel's revenue and profitability.

Revenue management is a critical business practice that hotels can utilize to maximize their revenue and profitability. It involves analyzing data and setting prices based on demand and other factors to optimize revenue. However, for a distressed hotel, revenue management becomes even more critical to its survival. A distressed hotel is one that is struggling to generate enough revenue to cover its expenses and make a profit. In this chapter, we will discuss revenue management strategies that can be implemented in a distressed hotel to turn it around and achieve profitability.

Section 1: Understanding the Market and Competition

The first step in implementing revenue management strategies in a distressed hotel is to understand the market and competition. This involves analyzing the hotel's location, target market, and competitors. By understanding these factors, the hotel can identify its unique selling points and develop a pricing strategy that is competitive and attractive to its target market.

For example, if the hotel is located in an area with many competitors, it may be challenging to attract guests. In this case, the hotel could differentiate itself by offering unique amenities, such as a spa, gym, or restaurant. By analyzing the competition, the hotel can identify areas where it can offer a better value proposition to guests.

Section 2: Understanding the Hotel's Demand

Once the hotel has a clear understanding of its market and competition, it needs to analyze its demand patterns. This involves collecting data on room bookings, cancellations, and no-shows to identify patterns and trends. The hotel can use this data to forecast demand and adjust its pricing strategy accordingly.

For example, if the hotel notices that bookings tend to peak during weekends, it can adjust its pricing strategy to capitalize on this trend. By offering discounts for midweek stays, the hotel can attract guests who are looking for a good deal and increase its occupancy rates.

Section 3: Managing Inventory

Inventory management is a critical aspect of revenue management. The hotel needs to manage its inventory of rooms effectively to maximize revenue. This involves setting different prices for different room types, depending on the level of demand.

For example, during peak demand periods, the hotel can set higher prices for its premium rooms and lower prices for its standard rooms. This strategy allows the hotel to maximize revenue while ensuring that all of its rooms are occupied.

Section 4: Pricing Strategies

There are several pricing strategies that a distressed hotel can use to increase its revenue. These include:

4.1 Discounting

Discounting is a pricing strategy that involves offering lower prices to attract guests. This strategy can be effective for a distressed hotel, as it can help to fill empty rooms and generate revenue that would otherwise be lost.

For example, the hotel could offer discounts to guests who book their rooms in advance or stay for an extended period. The hotel could also offer discounts to guests who book directly through the hotel's website or loyalty program.

4.2 Dynamic Pricing

Dynamic pricing is a strategy that involves adjusting prices based on demand. This strategy is particularly effective for hotels that experience significant fluctuations in demand.

For example, if the hotel notices that bookings are low for a particular date, it can lower its prices to attract more guests. On the other hand, if demand is high, the hotel can increase its prices to maximize revenue.

4.3 Bundling

Bundling is a pricing strategy that involves combining products or services to create a package deal. This strategy can be effective for hotels that offer multiple amenities, such as a spa or restaurant.

For example, the hotel could offer a package that includes a room, breakfast, and a spa treatment. By bundling these products, the hotel can offer a more attractive deal to guests and increase its revenue.

Section 5: Marketing and Distribution

Marketing and distribution are critical components of revenue management. The hotel needs to ensure that it is marketing its services effectively and distributing them through the right channels to reach its target market.

5.1 Online Travel Agencies (OTAs)

Online Travel Agencies (OTAs) are a popular distribution channel for hotels. These platforms allow hotels to reach a wider audience and attract guests who may not have heard of the hotel otherwise. However, they also come with commission fees that can eat into the hotel's revenue.

For a distressed hotel, OTAs can be an effective

distribution channel, as they can help to fill empty rooms and generate revenue. However, the hotel needs to be strategic about how it uses OTAs to avoid high commission fees.

For example, the hotel could use OTAs to promote discounted rates during periods of low demand. By doing so, the hotel can attract guests who are looking for a good deal while still maintaining its revenue levels.

5.2 Direct Booking

Direct booking is an essential component of revenue management. By encouraging guests to book directly through the hotel's website, the hotel can avoid commission fees and keep more of its revenue.

For a distressed hotel, direct booking can be particularly effective, as it allows the hotel to maintain control over its pricing and inventory management. The hotel can also offer incentives to guests who book directly, such as discounts or loyalty points, to encourage more direct bookings.

5.3 Social Media

Social media is another effective marketing channel for hotels. By using platforms like Facebook, Instagram, and Twitter, the hotel can reach a wider audience and engage with potential guests.

For a distressed hotel, social media can be an

effective way to promote discounted rates and special offers. By creating engaging content that showcases the hotel's unique features and amenities, the hotel can attract guests who are looking for a good deal.

Section 6: Staff Training

Finally, staff training is an essential component of revenue management. The hotel needs to ensure that its staff understands the importance of revenue management and how they can contribute to the hotel's success.

For example, front desk staff should be trained to upsell guests on premium rooms or amenities. Housekeeping staff should be trained to identify opportunities to upsell guests on services like room service or laundry.

In conclusion, revenue management is a critical business practice that hotels can use to maximize their revenue and profitability. For a distressed hotel, revenue management becomes even more critical to its survival. By understanding the market and competition, analyzing demand patterns, managing inventory effectively, using the right pricing strategies, marketing and distributing effectively, and providing staff training, a distressed hotel can turn itself around and achieve profitability. It is essential for hotels to continuously analyze their revenue management strategies to ensure that they are effective and adapted to the changing market conditions.

Chapter 19

Offer Corporate Rates

Offering corporate rates can help hotels to attract business travelers and increase occupancy rates. This can include partnerships with local businesses and corporations.

Example: The Fairmont Washington, D.C. offers corporate rates to businesses in the area. This program has been successful in attracting business travelers to the hotel and increasing occupancy rates.

Offering corporate and business rates for a distressed hotel is essential to increase revenue and attract more customers. In today's competitive hospitality industry, it is important to find innovative ways to attract corporate clients and offer them value for their money. This chapter will discuss how to offer corporate and business rates for a distressed hotel. It will also provide examples of successful implementation of such strategies in the hospitality industry.

Corporate and business clients are important to

hotels because they offer a steady stream of revenue. These clients may need to travel frequently for business and require comfortable accommodations. Offering corporate and business rates can help hotels attract these clients and build a loyal customer base. However, offering these rates requires careful planning and execution to ensure that both the hotel and the client benefit.

Strategies for Offering Corporate and Business Rates

Understand the market

The first step in offering corporate and business rates is to understand the market. This involves researching the types of businesses that are likely to use the hotel's services and their requirements. For example, a hotel located near a convention center may attract corporate clients attending conferences and exhibitions. Alternatively, a hotel near an industrial park may attract business clients looking for accommodation during site visits.

Understanding the market can help hotels tailor their services and rates to meet the needs of their target clients. For example, a hotel that attracts corporate clients attending conferences may offer discounted rates during peak conference seasons to attract more business.

Offer value-added services

In addition to offering competitive rates, hotels

can attract corporate and business clients by offering value-added services. These could include free Wi-Fi, complimentary breakfast, free parking, or discounts on hotel amenities such as the spa or gym. These services can help differentiate the hotel from competitors and attract clients who are looking for more than just a place to sleep.

For example, the Hilton Garden Inn in Dubai offers business travelers a range of value-added services, including a complimentary airport shuttle, free Wi-Fi, and a 24-hour business center. These services are designed to cater to the needs of business travelers and make their stay more comfortable.

Develop a loyalty program

Developing a loyalty program is another effective way to attract corporate and business clients. A loyalty program rewards clients for their repeat business and can help build a loyal customer base. This can include discounts on room rates, free upgrades, or other benefits.

For example, the InterContinental Hotels Group (IHG) offers a loyalty program called IHG Rewards Club. Members of the program can earn points for their stays, which can be redeemed for free nights, airline miles, or other rewards. This program is designed to encourage repeat business and build customer loyalty.

Establish partnerships

Establishing partnerships with other businesses can also be an effective way to attract corporate and business clients. This could include partnering with airlines, rental car companies, or other travel-related businesses. These partnerships can help hotels offer packages that include accommodation, transportation, and other services at a discounted rate.

For example, the Marriott hotel chain has a partnership with United Airlines that allows members of their loyalty programs to earn miles when they stay at a Marriott hotel. This partnership helps both businesses attract more customers and offer value-added services to their clients.

Attend trade shows

Attending trade shows is another effective way to attract corporate and business clients. Trade shows offer an opportunity to meet with potential clients and showcase the hotel's services. This can help build relationships with businesses and attract clients who are attending the trade show.

For example, the Radisson Hotel Group regularly attends trade shows such as the Business Travel Show and the World Travel Market. These shows provide an opportunity to meet with potential clients and showcase the hotel's services to a targeted audience.

Develop a sales team

Developing a sales team is essential to attracting corporate and business clients. A sales team can focus on building relationships with potential clients and promoting the hotel's services to businesses. This team can also negotiate rates and develop customized packages to meet the needs of clients.

For example, the Four Seasons Hotels and Resorts have a dedicated sales team that focuses on attracting corporate and business clients. This team works closely with clients to understand their needs and develop customized packages that include discounted rates, value-added services, and other benefits.

Examples of Successful Implementation of Corporate and Business Rates

Marriott International

Marriott International is one of the world's largest hotel chains and has a strong focus on attracting corporate and business clients. The company has developed a loyalty program called Marriott Bonvoy that rewards members for their repeat business. Members can earn points for their stays that can be redeemed for free nights, room upgrades, or other rewards.

Marriott also offers customized packages for corporate clients that include discounted rates, free Wi-Fi, and other value-added services. These packages are designed to meet the specific needs of corporate clients and provide them with a comfortable and productive stay.

Hilton Worldwide

Hilton Worldwide is another hotel chain that has a strong focus on attracting corporate and business clients. The company offers a loyalty program called Hilton Honors that rewards members for their repeat business. Members can earn points for their stays that can be redeemed for free nights, room upgrades, or other rewards.

Hilton also offers customized packages for corporate clients that include discounted rates, free Wi-Fi, and other value-added services. The company also has a dedicated sales team that focuses on building relationships with corporate clients and promoting the hotel's services.

InterContinental Hotels Group (IHG)

InterContinental Hotels Group (IHG) is a global hotel chain that operates several brands, including InterContinental, Crowne Plaza, and Holiday Inn. The company offers a loyalty program called IHG Rewards Club that rewards members for their repeat business. Members can earn points for their stays that can be redeemed for free nights, airline miles, or other rewards.

IHG also offers customized packages for corporate clients that include discounted rates, free Wi-Fi, and other value-added services. The company has a dedicated sales team that works closely with corporate clients to understand their needs and develop customized packages that meet their specific requirements.

In conclusion, offering corporate and business rates for a distressed hotel is essential to increase revenue and attract more customers. Hotels that understand their target market, offer value-added services, develop loyalty programs, establish partnerships, attend trade shows, and develop a sales team are more likely to attract corporate and business clients. Examples of successful implementation of such strategies can be seen in hotel chains such as Marriott, Hilton, and IHG. By following these strategies, distressed hotels can attract more corporate and business clients and build a loyal customer base, thus increasing their revenue and improving their financial situation.

Chapter 20

Increase Direct Bookings

Direct bookings can help hotels to reduce their

dependence on third-party booking sites and increase profits. This can include offering incentives for guests who book directly with the hotel.

Example: The Peninsula Beverly Hills offers a special rate for guests who book directly with the hotel. This incentive has been successful in increasing direct bookings and reducing the hotel's reliance on third-party booking sites.

The hospitality industry is one of the most competitive and dynamic industries in the world. The success of a hotel depends on its ability to attract and retain customers, and in recent years, this has become even more important due to the rise of online travel agencies (OTAs) and their increasing dominance over hotel bookings. Many hotels are struggling to increase direct bookings, which can be a major challenge for a distressed hotel that needs to boost its revenue quickly.

This chapter will discuss how to increase direct bookings for a distressed hotel, and will provide examples of each statement. The essay will begin by discussing the importance of a website for a hotel, followed by the importance of search engine optimization (SEO) and online advertising. The essay will then move on to discuss the importance of customer reviews and social media, and finally, will conclude with a discussion of loyalty programs and direct marketing.

Importance of a website

A website is one of the most important marketing tools for a hotel. It is the first point of contact for potential customers, and it is the place where customers can learn about the hotel, its services, and its amenities. A website should be visually appealing, easy to navigate, and provide all the necessary information about the hotel.

Example: The Arden Hotel in Stratford-upon-Avon, UK

The Arden Hotel is a luxury hotel in Stratford-upon-Avon, UK. The hotel's website is visually appealing and easy to navigate. The website provides all the necessary information about the hotel, including its location, services, and amenities. The website also includes high-quality photographs of the hotel, which showcase the hotel's luxurious interior and beautiful surroundings.

Importance of search engine optimization (SEO)

Search engine optimization (SEO) is the process of optimizing a website so that it appears at the top of search engine results pages (SERPs) for relevant keywords. SEO is important because most people use search engines to find hotels, and the higher a hotel's website appears in the search engine results, the more likely it is that people will visit the hotel's website.

Example: The Broadmoor in Colorado Springs, USA

The Broadmoor is a luxury hotel in Colorado Springs, USA. The hotel's website is optimized for search engines, and as a result, it appears at the top of the search engine results pages for relevant keywords. This has resulted in a significant increase in direct bookings for the hotel.

Importance of online advertising

Online advertising is another important way to increase direct bookings for a hotel. Online advertising allows a hotel to reach a wider audience than it would be able to reach through other marketing channels, and it can be targeted to specific demographics.

Example: The Ritz-Carlton in New York, USA

The Ritz-Carlton is a luxury hotel in New York, USA. The hotel uses online advertising to promote its services and amenities to a wide audience. The hotel's online advertising campaigns are targeted to specific demographics, such as business travelers and luxury travelers, and as a result, they have been very successful in increasing direct bookings for the hotel.

Importance of customer reviews

Customer reviews are an important factor in a hotel's success. They provide potential customers with insight into the quality of a hotel's services and amenities, and they can be a major factor in a customer's decision to book a hotel.

Example: The Four Seasons in Sydney, Australia

The Four Seasons in Sydney, Australia is a luxury hotel that has received numerous positive reviews from customers. The hotel's website features these reviews prominently, which has helped to increase the hotel's credibility and trustworthiness among potential customers.

Importance of social media

Social media is another important marketing tool for a hotel. It allows a hotel to connect with potential customers and to promote its services and amenities to a wider audience. Social media also provides a platform for customers to share their experiences with the hotel, which can help to increase the hotel's visibility and reputation.

Example: The Grand Hyatt in Dubai, UAE

The Grand Hyatt in Dubai, UAE is a luxury hotel that has a strong presence on social media. The hotel uses social media to promote its services and amenities to a wide audience, and it also encourages customers to share their experiences with the hotel on social media. This has helped to increase the hotel's visibility and reputation, and it has also helped to increase direct bookings for the hotel.

Importance of loyalty programs

Loyalty programs are a great way to increase direct bookings for a hotel. They provide customers with incentives to book directly with the hotel, and they also provide the hotel with valuable customer data that can be used to improve its marketing efforts.

Example: The Marriott Bonvoy program

The Marriott Bonvoy program is a loyalty program that is used by the Marriott hotel chain. The program provides customers with a range of benefits, including discounts on room rates, free Wi-Fi, and late checkout. These benefits provide customers with incentives to book directly with Marriott hotels, which helps to increase direct bookings for the hotels.

Importance of direct marketing

Direct marketing is another important way to increase direct bookings for a hotel. Direct marketing involves reaching out to potential customers directly, either through email, direct mail, or telemarketing.

Example: The Waldorf Astoria in Beverly Hills, USA

The Waldorf Astoria in Beverly Hills, USA uses direct marketing to promote its services and amenities to potential customers. The hotel sends out regular email newsletters to its subscribers, which include information about the hotel's latest offers and promotions. This has helped to increase direct bookings for the hotel, as customers are more likely to book directly with the hotel if they receive personalized offers and promotions.

In conclusion, increasing direct bookings for a distressed hotel can be a challenging task, but there are a number of strategies that can be used to achieve this goal. A website that is visually appealing and easy to navigate is essential, as is search engine optimization and online advertising. Customer reviews and social media are also important factors in a hotel's success, as they help to increase the hotel's visibility and reputation. Loyalty programs and direct marketing are additional strategies that can be used to increase direct bookings for a hotel. By implementing these strategies, a distressed hotel can increase its revenue and improve its chances of long-term success in the highly competitive hospitality industry.

Chapter 21

Offer flexible cancellation policies

Offering flexible cancellation policies can help hotels to attract more guests and improve customer satisfaction. This can include offering free cancellation up to a certain time before arrival.

Example: The InterContinental San Francisco offers a flexible cancellation policy that allows guests to cancel their reservation up to 24 hours before arrival. This policy has been successful in attracting more guests and improving customer satisfaction.

The hospitality industry is among the hardest hit by the COVID-19 pandemic. The crisis resulted in the closing of borders and restrictions in travel, which led to the collapse of the hotel industry. Hotels have to work hard to keep their doors open, and one of the ways to do this is by offering flexible cancellation policies. Flexible cancellation policies help hotels maintain bookings, keep guests satisfied, and ultimately increase revenue. This chapter discusses how hotels can offer flexible cancellation policies in the face of adversity using examples.

Flexible Cancellation Policies

A flexible cancellation policy is a policy that allows guests to cancel or modify their reservations without incurring charges. It is a vital tool for hotels to attract guests, especially in a market that is characterized by uncertainty. Guests feel more comfortable booking rooms knowing that they can cancel or modify their bookings without losing money. However, a flexible cancellation policy must be designed in a way that is sustainable for the hotel. Below are some ways in which hotels can offer flexible cancellation policies while still maintaining their financial viability.

Offer refundable and non-refundable rates

Offering refundable and non-refundable rates is a common strategy used by hotels to offer flexible cancellation policies. Refundable rates are more expensive than non-refundable rates because they give guests the flexibility to cancel their reservations without any penalties. On the other hand, non-refundable rates are cheaper but come with a catch; guests cannot cancel or modify their reservations. This strategy works well for hotels because it allows them to cater to guests with different needs. Guests who are more risk-averse may opt for the refundable rates, while those on a tight budget may go for the non-refundable rates. Additionally, hotels can set a deadline for the refundable rate; for example, guests may be allowed to cancel their reservation up to 24 hours before check-in.

The Four Seasons Hotels and Resorts is an example of a hotel chain that offers refundable and non-refundable rates. The chain has a "Book Early, Save More" promotion that allows guests to save up to 20% when they book their stays in advance. The promotion has both refundable and non-refundable rates, giving guests the option to choose what works for them.

Implement a sliding scale cancellation policy

A sliding scale cancellation policy is a policy that reduces the cancellation fee as the date of check-in approaches. This strategy is popular among hotels because it incentivizes guests to cancel early rather than wait until the last minute. For example, a hotel may charge 100% of the reservation fee if a guest cancels one day before check-in, but only 50% if the guest cancels two weeks before check-in. This strategy is effective because it allows hotels to maintain revenue while still offering guests some flexibility.

The Wyndham Hotels and Resorts is an example of a hotel chain that implements a sliding scale cancellation policy. The chain's cancellation policy states that guests will be charged a cancellation fee based on the number of days before check-in that they cancel. If guests cancel 30 or more days before check-in, they will not be charged a cancellation fee. However, if guests cancel within 24 hours of check-in, they will be charged 100% of the reservation fee.

Offer free cancellation within a specific timeframe

Offering free cancellation within a specific timeframe is a strategy that hotels can use to attract guests who are unsure of their travel plans. This strategy works well because it gives guests the option to cancel their reservations without any financial penalty, as long as they cancel within the specified timeframe. For example, a hotel may offer free cancellation up to seven days before check-in. This policy gives guests the flexibility to cancel their reservations if their plans change without incurring any charges.

The InterContinental Hotels Group is an example of a hotel chain that offers free cancellation within a specific timeframe. The chain's "Book Now, Pay Later" promotion allows guests to book their stays without paying upfront. The promotion has a free cancellation policy, where guests can cancel their reservations up to 24 hours before check-in without incurring any charges.

Implement a "Book Direct" policy

Implementing a "Book Direct" policy is a strategy that hotels can use to offer flexible cancellation policies while reducing their dependence on third-party booking platforms. Third-party booking platforms charge hotels a commission for every reservation made through their platforms, which can significantly reduce a hotel's revenue. By implementing a "Book Direct" policy, hotels can incentivize guests to book directly with them, which reduces the cost of acquiring customers and increases revenue. Additionally, hotels can use the savings from not paying commissions to offer more flexible cancellation policies to guests.

Marriott International is an example of a hotel chain that implements a "Book Direct" policy. The chain offers guests the lowest rates when they book directly with Marriott. Additionally, Marriott's loyalty program members enjoy even more benefits, including free Wi-Fi, exclusive rates, and free room upgrades. By incentivizing guests to book directly with Marriott, the chain reduces its dependence on third-party booking platforms and can offer more flexible cancellation policies to guests.

In conclusion, Flexible cancellation policies are a vital tool for hotels to maintain revenue and keep guests satisfied, especially in a market that is characterized by uncertainty. Hotels can offer flexible cancellation policies in several ways, including offering refundable and non-refundable rates, implementing a sliding scale cancellation policy, offering free cancellation within a specific timeframe, and implementing a "Book Direct" policy. However, hotels must design their flexible cancellation policies in a way that is sustainable for their business. Hotels that offer too much flexibility may find themselves in a situation where they are unable to maintain their financial viability. Overall, offering flexible cancellation policies is a balancing act between keeping guests satisfied and maintaining financial viability.

Chapter 22

Implement mobile technology

Mobile technology can help hotels to improve the guest experience and increase efficiency. This can include mobile check-in, keyless entry, and mobile concierge services.

Example: The Marriott Marquis in Houston implemented a mobile check-in system that allows guests to check in and receive their room key on their mobile device. This technology has helped to improve the guest experience and increase efficiency.

The hospitality industry has been one of the hardest hit industries in the world due to the COVID-19 pandemic. Hotels have been forced to change their operations and procedures to comply with health regulations and to ensure the safety of guests and staff. One of the solutions that many hotels have adopted is the use of mobile technology to improve guest experiences and streamline operations. This chapter will discuss how to implement mobile technology for a distressed hotel while using examples of each statement.

Statement 1: Understanding the Needs of Guests

The first step in implementing mobile technology for a distressed hotel is to understand the needs of guests. This involves conducting research to identify the challenges guests face when staying at the hotel and determining how mobile technology can help address these challenges. One of the main challenges that guests face is the need for contactless interactions to minimize the risk of infection. Mobile technology can help address this challenge by providing guests with the ability to perform tasks such as check-in, check-out, and room service orders through their mobile devices.

An example of a hotel that has successfully implemented mobile technology to address this challenge is the Hilton Honors app. The app allows guests to check-in and check-out of their rooms, order room service, and request housekeeping services using their mobile devices. This eliminates the need for guests to interact with staff in person, reducing the risk of infection. The app also allows guests to choose their preferred room and provides a digital key that allows them to access their room without interacting with staff.

Statement 2: Ensuring Compatibility with Existing Systems

The second step in implementing mobile technology for a distressed hotel is to ensure compatibility with existing systems. This involves conducting a thorough review of the hotel's current technology infrastructure and identifying any potential compatibility issues that may arise when implementing mobile technology. It is important to ensure that the mobile technology is compatible with the hotel's property management system (PMS) and other software applications that the hotel uses to manage its operations.

An example of a hotel that has successfully implemented mobile technology while ensuring compatibility with existing systems is the Marriott

Bonvoy app. The app integrates with Marriott's existing PMS and allows guests to check-in and check-out of their rooms, order room service, and request housekeeping services using their mobile devices. The app also provides guests with access to information about the hotel, including amenities, nearby attractions, and local restaurants.

Statement 3: Providing Personalized Experiences

The third step in implementing mobile technology for a distressed hotel is to provide personalized experiences. This involves using mobile technology to gather data about guests' preferences and behaviors and using this data to provide customized experiences that meet their needs. Mobile technology can also be used to provide guests with recommendations for local attractions and activities based on their interests.

An example of a hotel that has successfully implemented mobile technology to provide personalized experiences is the Four Seasons app. The app allows guests to customize their experience by selecting room preferences, ordering room service, and requesting housekeeping services. The app also provides guests with recommendations for local attractions and activities based on their interests.

Statement 4: Empowering Staff with Mobile Technology

The fourth step in implementing mobile technology for a distressed hotel is to empower staff with mobile technology. This involves providing staff with the tools they need to manage their tasks efficiently and effectively. Mobile technology can be used to automate tasks such as room service orders and housekeeping requests, freeing up staff to focus on more complex tasks such as guest interactions and problem-solving.

An example of a hotel that has successfully implemented mobile technology to empower staff is the Ritz-Carlton app. The app allows staff to manage tasks such as room service orders, housekeeping requests, and maintenance issues using their mobile devices. This eliminates the need for staff to physically visit the front desk to receive instructions, freeing up staff to focus on guest interactions and problem-solving.

Statement 5: Ensuring Data Security and Privacy

The fifth step in implementing mobile technology for a distressed hotel is to ensure data security and privacy. This involves implementing measures to protect guests' personal and financial information and to ensure that this information is not misused or disclosed without the guest's consent. Mobile technology can be vulnerable to cyberattacks and other security threats, so it is important to implement robust security measures to protect guests' data.

An example of a hotel that has successfully implemented mobile technology while ensuring data security and privacy is the InterContinental Hotels Group (IHG) app. The app uses industry-standard encryption to protect guests' personal and financial information and provides guests with the ability to set a PIN to secure their account. The app also allows guests to control their data privacy settings and provides clear information about how their data is collected and used.

Statement 6: Providing Continuous Support and Maintenance

The final step in implementing mobile technology for a distressed hotel is to provide continuous support and maintenance. This involves monitoring the performance of the mobile technology and addressing any issues that arise in a timely manner. It is also important to provide guests with support and assistance if they experience any issues with the mobile technology.

An example of a hotel that has successfully implemented mobile technology while providing continuous support and maintenance is the AccorHotels app. The app provides guests with access to a 24/7 support team that can assist with any issues they encounter while using the app. The app also provides guests with information about the hotel's policies and procedures, such as check-in and check-out times, and allows guests to make changes to their reservations as needed.

In conclusion, mobile technology can be a valuable tool for distressed hotels looking to improve guest experiences and streamline operations. To successfully implement mobile technology, hotels need to understand the needs of their guests, ensure compatibility with existing systems, provide personalized experiences, empower staff with mobile technology, ensure data security and privacy, and provide continuous support and maintenance. By following these steps and using examples of successful mobile technology implementations in the hospitality industry, distressed hotels can improve their operations and provide guests with a safe and enjoyable stay.

Chapter 23

Offer unique experiences

Offering unique experiences can help hotels to attract more guests and improve their reputation. This can include unique tours, classes, and events.

Example: The Westin Maui Resort & Spa offers a "Heavenly Honeymoon" package that includes a romantic sunset dinner and a couples massage. This unique experience has been successful in attracting more guests to the hotel.

The hotel industry is one of the most competitive industries, with hotels trying to offer unique and memorable experiences to their guests. The COVID-19 pandemic has caused unprecedented distress to the hotel industry, leading to declining revenues, occupancy rates, and cancellations. Hotels need to think outside the box to offer unique experiences to guests, especially during these challenging times. In this chapter, I will discuss how hotels can offer unique experiences for a distressed hotel by using examples of each statement.

Personalization

Personalization is an essential aspect of the hospitality industry, as guests expect personalized services and experiences. A personalized experience helps hotels to build strong relationships with guests and increase customer loyalty. Personalization can be achieved by understanding guest preferences, providing customized services, and anticipating guest needs.

Example: Four Seasons Hotel George V, Paris

The Four Seasons Hotel George V in Paris is renowned for its personalized services. The hotel offers a "MyFS" program, which allows guests to customize their stay according to their preferences. The program allows guests to choose their preferred amenities, room temperature, lighting, and even the fragrance of their room. The hotel also offers a personal concierge service that caters to guests' needs and preferences, such as arranging airport transfers, restaurant reservations, and city tours.

Sustainability

Sustainability is becoming an essential aspect of the hospitality industry, as guests are becoming more environmentally conscious. Hotels can offer unique experiences by adopting sustainable practices that reduce their environmental footprint. Sustainable practices can include reducing energy consumption, using renewable energy sources, reducing waste, and promoting eco-friendly activities.

Example: Soneva Fushi, Maldives

Soneva Fushi is an eco-friendly resort in the Maldives that offers unique sustainable experiences. The resort is powered by solar energy and uses a desalination plant to provide clean water. The resort also has an organic garden that provides fresh produce for the restaurants, and the waste is composted to fertilize the garden. The resort also offers eco-friendly activities, such as snorkeling with a marine biologist, participating in coral reef restoration projects, and stargazing in the resort's observatory.

Technology

Technology is transforming the hospitality industry, and hotels can offer unique experiences by adopting innovative technologies that enhance the guest experience. Technology can include mobile apps, virtual reality, augmented reality, and artificial intelligence. Technology can improve the guest experience by offering seamless services, personalized recommendations, and interactive experiences.

Example: Henn-na Hotel, Japan

Henn-na Hotel in Japan is a futuristic hotel that uses robots to provide services to guests. The hotel has robot receptionists, porters, and even a dinosaur robot that welcomes guests. The hotel also uses facial recognition technology to check-in guests and provide access to their rooms. The hotel also uses a tablet-based control system that allows guests to control their room temperature, lighting, and entertainment options.

Local Culture

Hotels can offer unique experiences by promoting the local culture and traditions of the destination. Local culture can include cuisine, art, music, architecture, and history. Promoting the local culture can help hotels to differentiate themselves from their competitors and provide guests with a memorable and authentic experience.

Example: Aman Tokyo, Japan

Aman Tokyo is a luxury hotel in Tokyo that promotes the local culture of Japan. The hotel features traditional Japanese architecture, including a Japanese garden and a Japanese tea room. The hotel also offers a "Kaiseki" dining experience, which is a traditional multi-course Japanese meal. The hotel also has an art gallery that features Japanese contemporary art and hosts exhibitions and events that promote the local culture.

Wellness

Wellness is becoming an essential aspect of the hospitality industry, as guests are becoming more health-conscious. Hotels can offer unique experiences by providing wellness facilities and services that promote health and well-being. Wellness can include spa treatments, fitness facilities, healthy cuisine, and wellness activities such as yoga, meditation, and mindfulness.

Example: COMO Shambhala Estate, Bali

COMO Shambhala Estate in Bali is a wellness retreat that offers unique experiences for guests seeking relaxation and rejuvenation. The retreat offers a range of wellness activities, including yoga, meditation, and Pilates. The retreat also has a spa that offers a range of treatments, including Ayurvedic therapies, massages, and facials. The retreat also offers healthy cuisine, with a focus on locally sourced, organic ingredients.

Adventure

Hotels can offer unique experiences by providing guests with adventurous activities and experiences. Adventure can include outdoor activities such as hiking, mountain biking, skiing, and water sports. Adventure can also include cultural experiences such as visiting local markets, attending cultural festivals, and participating in traditional activities.

Example: Explora Patagonia, Chile

Explora Patagonia in Chile is a hotel that offers unique adventure experiences for guests. The hotel is located in Torres del Paine National Park, a UNESCO Biosphere Reserve. The hotel offers a range of outdoor activities, including hiking, mountain biking, and horseback riding. The hotel also offers guided excursions to explore the natural beauty of the park, such as visiting glaciers, waterfalls, and lakes. The hotel also offers cultural experiences, such as visiting local ranches and learning about the traditional way of life in Patagonia.

Exclusivity

Hotels can offer unique experiences by providing guests with exclusive and luxurious experiences. Exclusivity can include private villas, personalized services, and exclusive access to facilities and activities. Exclusivity can help hotels to differentiate themselves from their competitors and provide guests with a sense of exclusivity and luxury.

Example: Amanzoe, Greece

Amanzoe is a luxury resort in Greece that offers exclusive experiences for guests seeking privacy and luxury. The resort features private villas that offer breathtaking views of the Aegean Sea. The resort also offers personalized services, including a private chef and a personal assistant. The resort also has an exclusive beach club that is only accessible to guests, offering a private beach, a pool, and a restaurant.

In conclusion, hotels can offer unique experiences by adopting various strategies, including personalization, sustainability, technology, local culture, wellness, adventure, and exclusivity. These strategies can help hotels to differentiate themselves from their competitors, provide guests with memorable and authentic experiences, and increase customer loyalty. The examples discussed in this essay demonstrate how hotels can offer unique experiences to their guests by adopting these strategies. The hospitality industry is continuously evolving, and hotels need to stay ahead of the game by innovating and adapting to changing guest expectations and preferences.

Chapter 24

Implement sustainable practices

Implementing sustainable practices can help hotels to reduce their environmental impact and improve their reputation. This can include reducing waste, conserving water, and using renewable energy sources.

Example: The Waldorf Astoria in New York City implemented a sustainability program that includes reducing waste and using renewable energy sources. This program has helped to improve the hotel's environmental impact and reputation.

Sustainable practices have become increasingly important in the hospitality industry due to their potential impact on the environment and the bottom line. The implementation of sustainable practices can not only reduce a hotel's carbon footprint, but also result in cost savings and improved guest satisfaction. However, for distressed hotels, the implementation of sustainable practices can pose a unique challenge due to limited resources and other pressing concerns. In this chapter, we will discuss how to implement sustainable practices for a distressed hotel using examples of each statement.

Assessment and Planning

The first step in implementing sustainable practices for a distressed hotel is to conduct an assessment of the hotel's current practices and identify areas where sustainable practices can be implemented. This assessment should take into account the hotel's physical infrastructure, energy and water usage, waste management, procurement practices, and employee engagement.

One example of a distressed hotel that successfully implemented sustainable practices through assessment and planning is the Hilton Vancouver Washington. In 2009, the hotel was facing declining occupancy rates and rising costs. To address these challenges, the hotel conducted an energy audit and identified several areas where energy efficiency improvements could be made. The hotel replaced inefficient lighting with LED bulbs, installed occupancy sensors in guest rooms, and implemented a program to encourage guests to reuse towels and linens. These efforts resulted in an annual savings of $50,000 in energy costs and a reduction in greenhouse gas emissions of 524 metric tons per year.

Energy Efficiency

Improving energy efficiency is one of the most effective ways for a distressed hotel to implement sustainable practices. There are several strategies that hotels can use to reduce energy usage, such as upgrading lighting systems, installing occupancy sensors, and implementing energy management systems.

One example of a hotel that successfully implemented energy efficiency improvements is the Marriott Marquis in Washington, D.C. The hotel conducted an energy audit and identified several areas where energy usage could be reduced. The hotel installed LED lighting in guest rooms and common areas, replaced old HVAC systems with more efficient models, and implemented an energy management system that automatically adjusts heating and cooling based on occupancy. These efforts resulted in an annual savings of $750,000 in energy costs and a reduction in greenhouse gas emissions of 3,800 metric tons per year.

Water Conservation

Another important area for implementing sustainable practices is water conservation. Hotels can implement several strategies to reduce water usage, such as installing low-flow showerheads and faucets, using water-efficient laundry equipment, and implementing water reuse systems.

An example of a hotel that successfully implemented water conservation practices is the Palazzo Hotel in Las Vegas. The hotel installed low-flow showerheads and faucets in guest rooms, implemented a program to encourage guests to reuse towels and linens, and installed a water-efficient laundry system. These efforts resulted in an annual savings of 60 million gallons of water and a reduction in greenhouse gas emissions of 9,000 metric tons per year.

Waste Management

Effective waste management is another important area for implementing sustainable practices.

Hotels can reduce waste by implementing recycling programs, composting food waste, and using eco-friendly products.

One example of a hotel that successfully implemented waste management practices is the Andaz Hotel in West Hollywood. The hotel implemented a recycling program for paper, plastic, and glass, composted food waste from the hotel's restaurant, and used eco-friendly cleaning products. These efforts resulted in an annual savings of $12,000 in waste disposal costs and a reduction in greenhouse gas emissions of 250 metric tons per year.

Procurement

Sustainable procurement practices can also help hotels reduce their environmental impact. Hotels can purchase products that are made from sustainable materials, have a low carbon footprint, and are produced using environmentally friendly practices.

An example of a hotel that successfully implemented sustainable procurement practices is the Fairmont Waterfront Hotel in Vancouver. The hotel implemented a sustainable seafood program that sources seafood from sustainable fisheries and aquaculture farms. The hotel also sources produce from local farms and uses eco-friendly cleaning products. These efforts resulted in an annual savings of $20,000 in procurement costs and a reduction in greenhouse gas emissions of 200 metric tons per year.

Employee Engagement

Finally, engaging employees in sustainable practices can help hotels achieve their sustainability goals. Employee engagement programs can include training on sustainable practices, recognition for sustainability achievements, and incentives for sustainable behavior.

An example of a hotel that successfully engaged employees in sustainable practices is the Hilton San Francisco Union Square. The hotel implemented a sustainability program that included training for employees on energy and water conservation, waste reduction, and sustainable procurement. The hotel also recognized employees who demonstrated sustainable behavior and provided incentives for sustainable practices, such as offering discounts for guests who opt out of daily housekeeping services. These efforts resulted in an annual savings of $500,000 in energy costs and a reduction in greenhouse gas emissions of 3,000 metric tons per year.

In conclusion, implementing sustainable practices for a distressed hotel can be a challenge, but it is also an opportunity to improve the hotel's bottom line and reduce its environmental impact. By conducting an assessment of current practices and implementing strategies for energy efficiency, water conservation, waste management, procurement, and employee engagement, hotels can achieve significant cost savings and environmental benefits. The examples discussed in this essay demonstrate that sustainable practices are feasible for all types of hotels, including those that are struggling financially. Ultimately, sustainable practices are not only good for the environment, but also for the long-term success of the hotel industry.

Chapter 25

Foster a positive company culture

Fostering a positive company culture can help hotels to improve employee morale and performance, which can ultimately lead to better guest experiences and financial performance. This can include offering employee training and development programs, recognition and rewards programs, and a supportive work environment.

Example: The Four Seasons Hotel in Toronto has a strong company culture that focuses on employee development and recognition. The hotel offers extensive training and development programs for employees, as well as a rewards and recognition program that highlights employee achievements. This positive company culture has helped to improve employee morale and performance, which has translated into better guest experiences and financial performance for the hotel.

Fostering a positive company culture is crucial for any business, but it becomes even more important in times of distress. A positive company culture can help to build resilience, increase employee engagement, and ultimately, lead to a more successful business. In this chapter, we will discuss how to foster a positive company culture for a distressed hotel. We will use examples to illustrate each statement and show how they can be applied in practice.

Communicate openly and transparently

Open and transparent communication is essential for creating a positive company culture, especially in a distressed hotel. Employees are often anxious and worried about their jobs during tough times, and clear communication can help alleviate some of their fears. Managers should be transparent about the state of the business and the steps they are taking to improve it. They should also encourage employees to share their concerns and ideas.

One example of open communication in a distressed hotel is the CEO of Marriott International, Arne Sorenson's video message to employees during the COVID-19 pandemic. In the video, he acknowledged the challenges faced by the hotel industry and the impact it was having on Marriott employees. He assured them that the company was doing everything possible to minimize job losses and support those who were affected. This level of open communication helped to build trust and confidence in Marriott's employees, even in the face of uncertainty.

Empower employees

Empowering employees is another important aspect of fostering a positive company culture. Employees who feel valued and trusted are more likely to be engaged and committed to their work. Managers should give employees the autonomy to make decisions and take ownership of their work. They should also provide training and development opportunities to help employees grow and succeed.

An example of empowering employees in a distressed hotel is the Four Seasons Hotel in New York City. During the COVID-19 pandemic, the hotel had to lay off most of its staff. However, instead of simply letting them go, the hotel offered a range of training programs and development opportunities to help employees upskill and prepare for future employment. This approach not only helped to retain the talent within the hotel but also showed a commitment to employee development and empowerment.

Foster a sense of community

A sense of community is crucial for building a

positive company culture, particularly in a distressed hotel. When employees feel like they are part of a community, they are more likely to be engaged and committed to their work. Managers should encourage employees to build relationships with each other, both inside and outside of work. They should also organize team-building activities and social events to foster a sense of community.

An example of fostering a sense of community in a distressed hotel is the Andaz Maui at Wailea Resort in Hawaii. During the COVID-19 pandemic, the hotel organized a range of activities and events to keep employees engaged and connected. These included virtual happy hours, cooking classes, and fitness challenges. By fostering a sense of community, the hotel was able to maintain employee morale and build a stronger team, even during difficult times.

Lead by example

Leadership is critical for creating a positive company culture, particularly in a distressed hotel. Managers should lead by example, demonstrating the values and behaviors they expect from their employees. They should also be visible and approachable, making themselves available to listen to feedback and concerns from employees.

An example of leading by example in a distressed hotel is the Ritz-Carlton Hotel in Boston. During the COVID-19 pandemic, the hotel's general manager,

Richard White, personally visited each employee to check in on their wellbeing and offer support. He also led by example, demonstrating a strong commitment to employee safety by implementing strict health and safety protocols. This approach helped to build trust and confidence in the hotel's leadership and showed a commitment to putting employee wellbeing first.

Recognize and reward good performance

Recognizing and rewarding good performance is a crucial aspect of fostering a positive company culture. When employees feel appreciated and valued, they are more likely to be engaged and motivated to perform at their best. Managers should regularly acknowledge and reward employees who perform well, whether it's through verbal recognition or more tangible rewards.

An example of recognizing and rewarding good performance in a distressed hotel is the Ace Hotel in New York City. During the COVID-19 pandemic, the hotel had to reduce its staff, but the remaining employees were given additional responsibilities and training to help them adapt to the changing circumstances. The hotel also implemented a recognition program to reward employees who went above and beyond in their roles. These rewards included bonuses, extra vacation days, and other incentives. By recognizing and rewarding good performance, the hotel was able to maintain high levels of employee engagement and commitment, even during challenging times.

Create a positive work environment

Creating a positive work environment is another important aspect of fostering a positive company culture. Managers should ensure that the workplace is safe, comfortable, and conducive to productivity. They should also encourage employees to personalize their workspaces and create a sense of ownership over their environment.

An example of creating a positive work environment in a distressed hotel is the Hilton London Bankside hotel. The hotel has a rooftop garden where employees can relax and take a break from their work. The hotel also provides comfortable workspaces with natural lighting and ergonomic furniture to help employees feel more comfortable and productive. By creating a positive work environment, the hotel was able to improve employee wellbeing and foster a more positive company culture.

Encourage work-life balance

Encouraging work-life balance is another important aspect of fostering a positive company culture, particularly in a distressed hotel where employees may be under increased stress and pressure. Managers should encourage employees to take breaks, prioritize their wellbeing, and maintain a healthy work-life balance. They should also offer flexible working arrangements where possible, such as remote work or flexible schedules.

An example of encouraging work-life balance in a distressed hotel is the Hyatt Regency McCormick Place hotel in Chicago. The hotel offers a range of employee benefits, including a fitness center, yoga classes, and a wellness program. The hotel also offers flexible scheduling and remote work options to help employees balance their work and personal commitments. By prioritizing employee wellbeing and work-life balance, the hotel was able to maintain high levels of employee engagement and commitment, even during challenging times.

In conclusion, fostering a positive company culture is crucial for any business, but it becomes even more important in times of distress. A positive company culture can help to build resilience, increase employee engagement, and ultimately, lead to a more successful business. In this essay, we have discussed seven ways to foster a positive company culture for a distressed hotel, using examples to illustrate each statement. By implementing these strategies, hotels can create a more positive and supportive work environment, even in the face of adversity.

Chapter 26

Conclusion

In conclusion, distressed hotel assets can present a significant challenge for hotel owners, but there are a variety of strategies that can be employed to turn the property around. By focusing on improving guest experiences, increasing occupancy rates, reducing costs, and improving financial performance, hotel owners can successfully turnaround a distressed asset. Examples of real hotels that have successfully implemented these strategies include The Plaza Hotel in New York City, The Westin St. Francis in San Francisco, and The Ritz-Carlton in New York City. Each of these hotels employed a variety of strategies to improve their financial performance and attract more guests, including renovations and updates, marketing and branding, sustainability initiatives, and employee development programs.

Overall, turning around a distressed hotel asset requires a multifaceted approach that considers all aspects of the hotel's operations. By implementing a combination of these strategies, hotel owners can improve their financial performance and create a sustainable business model that can thrive in the long term.